Acknowledgements

My deep appreciation to Susan and Jerry Machado for all their help in this and countless other adventures.

Thank you to my copyeditor, Jean Blomquist, for her sensitive work. To Leia Carlton, Dr. Benjamin Levine, Pacific Palisades Public Library, and to UCLA's Powell and University Research Libraries for their assistance.

A special acknowledgment and thanks to my contributors. Family and friends who were willing to share special moments and memories. Your stories add so much to the essence of the California spirit that I have tried to capture in this book.

To Mace and Carolyn Perlman and to Kelley White who understand and pass it on.

To my parents Oakley and Nita for everything, just everything. And you know how much that is—it's everything!

Most importantly, my thanks to Roy M. Carlisle, Editorial Director at Wildcat Canyon Press, for this opportunity—a California dream come true!

EDITOR'S NOTES:

1. Some contributors' names have been changed to protect their privacy.

2. The names of many of the products mentioned in these pages are registered trademarks, belonging to their owners. We fully acknowledge the rights of these owners.

Where We Came From

From a far country and times long ago, Europeans discovered this land from the sea.

Over four hundred years ago, a ship flying Spanish colors with commander Juan Rodriguez Cabríllo at the helm first sailed into what is now known as San Diego Bay. They were the first Europeans to discover the promise of California, where the forest meets the sea. This land offered the explorers not only a heavenly climate but fertile soil as well. California offered then what it offers today, promise—we are the state of hopes and dreams!

Immigrants spilled into California by land and by sea. They chose to settle in a land where the most diverse environment on earth also provided opportunities to live and work.

Olive orchards and citrus groves, fur trapping, logging, vineyards, whaling, ranching, railroad building and the rumor of that gold! Word spread quickly on how to get here and what to bring, and the folks came by the wagon- and boat-load.

When the rumor of gold became a fact with John Marshall's discovery in 1848, people rushed in from everywhere, dropping what they held in their hands, bringing with them only the clothes they wore. When the gold mines exploded, the population did too! People pushed forward, moving on to California, with a glitter in their eye and a dream in their hearts.

The high seas were busy as ships carrying people from all over the world poured in. Among the countries who sent their people were England, France, Russia, Italy, Africa, Japan, China, Scotland, and Ireland. Americans from states and territories to the east stampeded in as well.

Although the commodities have changed, the promise of our state remains the same. California offers health and wealth—the promise of a better life. We epitomize the American dream. This is a magical state that glitters and shines, where stars are found—and can fall.

The promise of California reaches far and wide calling out to the millions that love calling California home.

Who Was Here First

The Indians and a bristlecone pine.

The Native Americans were here about 12,000 years before sailors sailed and settlers settled. California's gorgeous climate and very inhabitable land was hidden from the sailors behind hillsides that rose from the sea and from the settlers by the Sierra Nevada Mountains. Although the exact number is not known, it is estimated that somewhere between two hundred and five hundred tribes lived within the bounds of California before the Spanish arrived.

★　★　★

In Inyo National Forest, located on the eastern escarpment of the Sierra Nevada, grows a bristlecone pine that is thought to be more than 4,500 years old, making it the OLDEST living thing on earth.

General Sherman, a redwood in Sequoia National Park, stands more than 270 feet tall, with a base circumference of over 100 feet, making it the LARGEST living thing on earth. Someone figured out that the tree would make 5,000,000,000 matches or forty-five-room houses.

Imperial County is a prehistoric wonderland. A group of huge animal footprints near the Fish Creek Mountains lead to a water hole where mastodons came to drink.

How many holes can a woodpecker peck in an old yellow pine in the San Jacinto Mountains? 31,800.

One of the grandest sights in the western United States are the groves of indigenous date palms near the world-famous resort of Palm Springs. In the Palm, Andreas, and Murray Canyons, the Washingtonia palms are estimated to be 1,500 to 2,000 years old.

The Indians derived their medicines from plants and herbs. A shaman sometimes treated the ailing. Homeopathic and other alternative methods of treatment continue and thrive in California today.

Riverside County is exceptionally rich in prehistoric Indian rock writing. The mysterious petroglyphs and pictographs depict stories of fires, hunts, and battles. Some of the most inexplicable of these relics, best seen from the air, are located seventeen miles north of Blythe, near the Colorado River. Both humans and animals are represented; the largest is a human figure 167 feet long. These ancient drawings earned the site a place on the National Register of Historic Places.

The California Chumash Indians made beads from oyster and abalone shells. They used them for money, which introduced the concept of currency to North America. Chumash women were avid gamblers, tossing dice across a flat, coiled basket-tray. The men did not farm, but they were great hunters. They used bows and arrows, javelins, clubs, slings, curved throwing sticks, and traps. They were expert marksmen.

Pomo Indians wove baskets from native reeds so tight they were watertight! In addition they were fireproof when used for cooking over an open fire.

The Hoopa Valley Reservation in Humboldt County is the most populated of the 109 statewide Indian reservations in California.

California Indians lived through a system of cooperative decision making. Food was plentiful and the climate so good that the Indians of California, like the Californians of today, were able to enjoy a great deal of leisure.

Native California is broken into territories similarly as it is into counties. There are fifty-seven native territories and fifty-eight counties. The different sections indicate tribe names. In the northern part of the state, the territories are smaller and more condensed.

Some of those names are:

Yana	Tolowa	Achumawi	Modoc	Maidu
Yurok	Pomo	Chimiriko	Atsugewi	
Hupa	Nisenan	Coast Miwok	Yuki	

In the central section of the state:

| Miwok | Paiute | Ohlone | Yokuts | Tubatulabal |
| Shoshone | Mono | Chumash | Salinan | |

In southern California:

| Mohave | Chemehuevi | Serrano | Tataviam | Tongva |
| Kumeyaay | Cahuilla | Ajachmen | Halchidhoma | Yuma |

Who Came

Given the very density and diversity of contemporary California's population, it is difficult to imagine how it got that way. But it started somewhere, and the following glimpse at who arrived after the Indians makes threading a common history between Californians a little easier.

How did California come to be known as the Golden State? To mark their way, the men traveling overland spread mustard seeds which then mixed with the indigenous poppies, creating the golden fields of wildflowers that cover our hills and roadsides.

French, Russian, Spanish, Mexican, English, and American were among the visitors who traveled back and forth hoping to seize and occupy, astonished at the magnificence and opportunity awaiting them. During those years, word of a magical Garden of Eden—California—continued to spread throughout parts of Europe and Asia, especially China. And the people came. Many different countries were on a similar course of discovery at approximately the same time.

Of course we already know why people love California—after all, we live here! But taking a look at the first influx of settlers helps to establish the ethnic diversity that continues to thrive today. Dreamers and promise seekers came by land and by sea to call this fabled region home. California was compelling and exciting even then—offering the promise of a better life—and you can't keep people from seeking their dreams.

"Know now, then, that, on the right hand of the Indies, there is an island called California, very close to the side of the Terrestrial Paradise, and it was peopled by black women, without any man among them, for they lived in the fashion of Amazons. They were of strong and hardy bodies, of ardent courage and great force. Their island was the strongest in all the world, with its steep cliffs and rocky shores. Their arms were all of gold, and so was the harness of the wild beasts which they tamed and rode. For, in the whole island, there was no metal but gold. They lived in caves wrought out of the rock with much labor. They had many ships which they sailed out to other countries to obtain booty.

"In this island, called California, there were many griffins, on account of the great ruggedness of the country, and its infinite host of wild beasts, such as never were seen in any other part of the world . . . and their Queen was called Calif."

GRACE RODRIQUEZ ORDÓÑEZ DE MONTALUO
From the novel *Las Sergas de Esplandían,* circa 1510
(The Exploits of Esplandían)

Here is a date that may look familiar:

September 28, 1542. Commander Juan Rodriguez Cabríllo first sailed in to the bay of San Miguel. Sixty years later Sebastián Vizcaíno entered the same port and named it Bay of San Diego.

During his global circumnavigation in 1579, Sir Francis Drake, from England, claimed California "Nova Albion." "Albion" was the ancient name for Great Britain and "Nova" means new. According to some Drake had stopped for repairs in what is now known as Drakes Bay (Point Reyes) and left a brass plate that read:

IN THE NAME OF HERR MAIESTY QVEEN ELIZABETH OF ENGLAND AND HERR SVCCESSORS FOREVER. But the authenticity of the plate has been questioned.

The Royal French Navy sent Jean François Galoup de LaPérouse on a round-the-world expedition. In September of 1786, to replenish his supplies for a voyage to the Philippines, he anchored in Monterey Bay.

On his way to China from Boston, Ebenezer Dorr, captain of the Otter, sailed into Monterey Bay for water and wood in 1796. From the late 1790s onward, many American trading ships operated off the coast of California.

Count Nikolai Petrovich Reszanov, a Russian, dreamed of establishing a Russian California after sailing into San Francisco Bay in 1806. His intention was to expand "Russian American" southward from Alaska.

Three years later, in 1809, another Russian voyage, led by Ivan Alexander Kuskov, reached Bodega Bay. He later founded a colony at Fort Ross in Sonoma County and began trading sea otter pelts. Also at Fort Ross, the Russians established California's first commercial shipyard where they built vessels for the Spanish.

John Gilroy from Scotland jumped ship at Monterey in 1814 and decided to stay. The city of Gilroy is known for its annual Garlic Festival and is named after, you guessed it, John Gilroy.

The French left their influence many years later in 1831, when Jean-Louis Vignes from the Bordeaux region, arrived in Los Angeles carrying a supply of grape cuttings. California's first fine wine tasting took place at Union Station in Los Angeles. Vignes dedicated the next thirty years to his California vineyards.

After living in Mexico for six years Hugo Reid arrived in California in 1834. He met and married Doña Victoria, a widowed Gabrieleno Indian and heiress to Rancho Santa Anita in the San Gabriel Valley. His new wife was the wealthiest woman in the state.

The African grandparents of Maria Rita Valdez were among the founders of Los Angeles. They owned Rancho Rodeo de Las Aguas, better known today as Beverly Hills.

Another African American, Francisco Reyes, owned the San Fernando Valley. Later he sold it and became mayor of Los Angeles.

Peter Lassen, from Denmark, came to California as a blacksmith and befriended John Sutter. Although Lassen died in poverty, his contemporaries thought highly of him and bestowed many things with his name including a national park, a forest, and a volcano—all in Lassen County.

Here come the Irish pioneers: John Reed began logging the Corte Madera redwoods in what is now Marin County. A small Irish community soon developed.

German-born Jacob Reese built San Francisco's first permanent house. Did you know that Anaheim is a German name? "Ana" stands for the Santa Ana River and "heim" means "home" in German.

John Sutter, from Switzerland, developed New Helvetia, a colony near Sacramento. More to come about John Sutter. Think gold nuggets.

William Leidesdorff, whose father was Danish and mother African, was born in the Virgin Islands. He was the first African American pioneer in San Francisco and arrived already wealthy. Leidesdorff shortly became involved with and influential in the effort to make California part of the United States. He was appointed a U.S. sub-consul, probably making him the first African American diplomat in the nation's history. He made yet another fortune in shipping, lumber, and real estate, and thus became California's first million-aire. Leidesdorff died in 1848. Large numbers of African Americans from the South came to California because California was an anti-slavery state. Within a ten-year time block, the number of African Americans in California jumped from 124,000 to 462,000.

Today seventy-two percent of all Chinese in the United States live in California.

As we approached the end of the twentieth century, new popula-tion movements were occurring. People from Arabia, Armenia, Vietnam, Korea, and Cambodia continued to add pockets of color and sprinkle new dimensions to the heterogeneous mix. People from countries all across the planet are represented in California today. Just about anywhere one goes, whether it be the businesses that we support, a walk through a neighborhood, a drive across town, or the close quarters of apartment living, the international flavor of California can be experienced by everyone calling Califor-nia home.

The Great Discovery

1848. The same year that California officially becomes a part of the United States, gold is discovered!

★　★　★

From the man who made the rumors real, James Marshall, comes one of the most famous sentences in California history:

My eye was caught by something shining in the bottom of the ditch. I reached my hand down and picked it up; it made my heart thump, for I was certain that it was gold. The piece was about half the size and shape of a pea. Then I saw another . . . .

The first flurry of news was spread when Sam Brannan, owner of *The California Star* in San Francisco, held out his bottle of gold, startling passers-by as he shouted:

Gold. Gold! GOLD! In the American River!

Possibly the most frequently quoted paragraph in the state's history:

The blacksmith dropped his hammer, the carpenter his plane, the mason his trowel, the farmer his sickle, the baker his loaf, and the tapster his bottle. All were off for the mines, some on horses, some on carts, and one on crutches, and one went in a litter. An American woman, who had recently established a boarding-house here, pulled up stakes, and was off before her lodgers had even time to pay their bills. Debtors ran, of course. I have only a community of women left and a gang of prisoners, with here and there a soldier

who will give his captain the slip at first chance. I don't blame the fellow a whit; seven dollars a month, while others making two or three hundred a day!

WALTER COLTON
Monterey leader and naval chaplain

The accounts of the abundance of gold in that territory are of such an extraordinary character as would scarcely command belief were they not corroborated by the authentic reports of officers in the public service.

PRESIDENT JAMES K. POLK, Washington, DC
State of the Union message

ONCE UPON A TIME . . . BUT TRUE . . .
THE GOLD RUSH

WOULDN'T YOU KNOW IT, once gold was discovered in California the news spread quicker than ours does today with e-mail, faxes, and telephones. Well, not really, but taking into consideration that the methods of transmission in those days were horse, hand, ship, and word of mouth, the reaction was nearly instantaneous.

John Marshall carried the first gold nuggets to John Sutter, at Sutter's Fort, to test the material and make sure it held up. You know it did, and although they urged the other workers at the fort to maintain the secrecy of their find, excitement of this kind—a revelation this extraordinary—was impossible to hush for long! This was electrifying news, a touch of magic, when our not-so-distant relatives during those pioneering days of yore broke ground and made headway. The times were wild, reckless, and free.

Certainly no other event prior, and possibly since, has had a greater influence upon the progress and expansion of our country than the discovery of gold in California. The California gold rush sparked the largest mass migration in history.

★   ★   ★

Word traveled north to Oregon where over half of the male population fled.

Vaqueros were harassed by bandits and Indians as they traveled from southern California with cattle and canvas sacks stuffed with gold slugs.

The most sterling families from the East sent their most educated sons.

Among the newcomers were African Americans. Some were slaves who came from the Southern states to work in the mines and used their earnings to buy their freedom.

The vicinity of San Ramón was primarily full of Irish. So much so that the area was known as Lynchville and nicknamed Limerick.

Mifflin Gibbs, born in Philadelphia, established the first African American newspaper in California, *Mirror of the Times*. Years later, in 1873, in Little Rock, Arkansas, he was elected a city judge.

Forty thousand promise seekers who all shared the same dream of a better life stampeded into California. The majority of them were young, healthy, white, male, and Protestant. The California Trail alone endured the passage of 1,500 horsemen and 6,200 wagons carrying upward of 35,000 people.

People poured into California. All byways were gridlocked. The first traffic jam was underway! Trading vessels carried word off in every direction through Los Angeles and Mexico, Chile and Peru. The high seas were busy. Upward of seven hundred vessels carrying immigrants from all over the globe sailed into the San Francisco Bay.

The year was 1849 and these were the forty-niners.

How They Lived

They didn't call it the Wild West for nothing. Wild it was. California was rugged, undeveloped, and difficult to reach. Men lived either alone or with each other, leaving their families back home. When the times and attitudes changed from California dreaming to California settling, some order was restored as women followed their men west. They established homes and new lives for their husbands and children, and with them, civility and culture followed.

Those old timers were rough, tough, and living in times when brawn counted for more than brains. Some lived outdoors, preferring to move rather than hang their hat, when the call of the wild and a shot in the dark ruled the night.

Crouching along a cold river's stream with the scorching-hot sun overhead, the miners were ever alert for the swirl of gold in their pans. Why, sometimes it poured through their very hands! Every dip of the tin held within it a gamble—because if luck smiled, so then did the future. At the end of the day, the cost of all that freedom was high as men fell to the ground exhausted, filthy, and starving. They never knew, with each stroke of the pick, what it may bring forth. It was exactly this excitement and fascination that enabled them to endure many of the hardships that they did.

About the only thing they had too much of was whiskey: dead drunk and flat broke one day, then moving on and setting up camp somewhere else the next. They cooked their own grub, washed their own shirts, and sewed their own buttons, while they hollered and fought among themselves in frustration and fear. Gambling dens and saloons were not far away.

Ramshackle camps or shantytowns with primitive sanitation and untended streets sprang up. Improving matters meant losing time—and that meant losing money. People endured nearly intolerable conditions. If any facilities to care for the sick or injured were available, they were crude and filthy.

As the land continued to provide gold and more riches were claimed, prices skyrocketed. A dozen eggs fetched $10.00, and an apple sometimes cost $2.00.

Many old wooden buildings were built with iron shutters and winding, outdoor stairways. Because of dryness and heat, fires were common. Soon wood was replaced with adobe or brick. Many little towns had a Main Street, a jail and a courthouse, a shave shop, and a town store.

Men living as outlaws congregated in Los Angeles, while at the same time, Anglo-Mexican-Indian animosities continued. Pistols and rifles were a way of life, as rustlers preyed on livestock and vigilantes ambushed. Outlaw gangs brawled with desperadoes; drunken men and women woke up in jail. These were the days of the Wild West!

★   ★   ★

What Was a Fellow Without a Female?

WOMEN WERE SO RARE that the miners often did not even see one for months at a time.

With nothing feminine anywhere, how homesick those fellows must have been for their wives, women, and children—the lives they had left behind. No disappointment was quite so bad as when the postmaster passed them by without handing over an expected letter. With an aching gaze up under the stars or a fixed stare into the campfire, the most lonesome sounds of all were the voices of the night: the owls, the frogs, the sigh in the pines, or a coyote howling at a faraway moon. The men wondered if they were missed at all.

★   ★   ★

More than half of all Californians in 1850 were males in their twenties, a time when desire for female companionship is at its peak, yet only one in thirty Californians was a woman in the same age bracket.

Female population in some mining camps was one percent.

Out of 15,000 Chinese to arrive in San Francisco, only seven were women.

Women arriving in California were received as heroes. In the boomtown of Downieville, the first female to arrive drew out the entire male population who then escorted her through town in a parade.

Three hundred Italian miners walked nine miles to see one Italian immigrant woman.

The yearning was everywhere, even in the songs they wrote:

>Oh Sally, dearest Sally,
>Oh Sally, for your sake,
>I'll go to Californy'
>An' try to raise a stake.

Waiting for the return of their husbands and fathers, women and children had stayed back home. But not for long. The year 1852 experienced the arrival of more people in California than any preceding year! Why? Those women and children missed their husbands and their papas! Attitudes were changing as homeseekers, not just promise seekers, made their way west as well.

I'M ROUGH AND I'M TOUGH AND I DON'T WEAR BLOOMERS

THERE HAS BEEN A LOT OF TALK up to now about men. Where do the ladies come in during all of this? Everyone had a rough go of it back then. After all, they weren't staying at the local motel as they traveled over the hills and across the land. It was either hot or cold, and it was always dirty. They didn't even have the luxury of running water on those bumpy and excruciating trips.

The women had children, and they held down the fort. In the big cities, they were making early progress and bringing home the bacon, while women back home on the range fried it up in the pan. If the quotes below are any indication of how they managed it all, they did so with wisdom and humor.

Native Americans believe that everything in the world is alive the same way that humans are alive.

These baskets are alive.
– Fanny Flounder, 1900

In San Francisco, in order to find themselves better jobs, women organized a Ladies Protection Relief Society.

Oakland's first weekly newspaper was *The Contra Costa,* and Sara Moore Clarke became the publisher in 1854.

A women's magazine, *The Hesperian,* received the Certificate of Merit at the Industrial Exposition in San Francisco.

The way to avoid housework is to live outside.
– Sandra Blacksmith, 1900

Indian chiefs could be either male or female. They were chosen not on their power to control, but rather on their ability to get everyone to agree. What a concept!

There is no safety out here on the Plains. If it's not the wind, it'll be something else.
– Mrs. Colby Penn, 1865

A good-looking pair of legs beats a pair of sixes.
– Jody Bell, 1886

Cussing like a sailor with a patch over one missing eye and his teeth destroyed by tobacco, the loner and stagecoach driver out of San Francisco was named "Cockeyed" Charley Parkhurst. When Parkhurst died, the astonished undertaker discovered that ol' Cockeyed Charley was born Charlotte—a woman!

When I was a girl, I had dreams of becoming a woman. Now that I'm a woman, I have dreams of becoming a girl.
– AGNES MOBLEY, 1898

Keep neat and clean, avoid bad habits, be faithful, and never take . . . from anyone.
– ROSE WHITE, 1886

Emily Pitts Stevens owned the *Sunday Evening Mercury,* and in her front-page editorials she supported what were then feminist causes: the eight-hour work day and women's right to vote.

I don't have room on my face for one more character line.
– AMANDA DAVIS, 1887

Horticulturist Eliza Tibbits of Riverside was sent navel orange trees by the U.S. Department of Agriculture. The trees won awards at major expositions for their superior taste and quality. Soon Mrs. Tibbets had a booming blooming business that generated millions of dollars in the citrus industry.

If you do a foolish thing, do it like you mean it.
– SARAH BLACKSMITH, 1900

The last time I rode the trail with a band of outlaws, I fell in love with three of them.
– CHARLOTT LARSON, 1905

The pioneering spirit of the women's movement started 127 years ago, in 1871, when the first Pacific Coast Woman Suffrage Convention took place in San Francisco. Forty years later, in 1911, all Americans had the right to vote.

A 1986 California survey showed that over half of Californians with assets over $500,000 were women.

THE NUMBERS GAME

California is home to immigrants from every corner of this planet. Take a look at our state's population by ancestry. From a U.S. census in 1990, here are the top twenty:

1. Mexican	11. Polish
2. German	12. Swedish
3. English	13. Salvadorian
4. Irish	14. Dutch
5. Italian	15. Russian
6. Filipino	16. Japanese
7. Chinese	17. Vietnamese
8. French	18. Portuguese
9. Scottish-Irish	19. Norwegian
10. Scottish	20. Korean

Church Membership in California

The American way is rooted in personal freedom, which is integral to the California dream. Along with so many diverse lifestyles comes diverse belief systems, and California has always been open-minded to alternative ways of doing things. Sometimes viewed as flaky, occasionally dismissed by the more traditional areas of the nation, California offers more independent religious organizations than in the rest of the nation combined! We have been a laboratory of sorts, a testing ground. We are progressive and controversial because of it. This proliferation of faiths is by now a cultural tradition. Take what you like and leave the rest, what makes California so refreshing is that we welcome all.

The top ten most practiced faiths:

1. Roman Catholic
2. Baptist
3. Methodist
4. Lutheran
5. Presbyterian
6. Jewish
7. Mormon
8. Episcopalian
9. Pentecostal
10. Other faiths

California Catholics have 15 universities, 117 high schools, 598 elementary schools.

And here is a look at a few churches found in Fresno and Los Angeles.

Fresno	Los Angeles
Lao First Baptist Church	Church of Religious Science
Sikh Association of Fresno	Self-Realization Fellowship
Hmong Baptist Mission	First African Methodist Church
Greek Orthodox Church	Chinese Bible Church
Pilgrim Armenian Church	Los Angeles Buddhist Church
Indonesia Full Gospel Fellowship	Infinite Science Church
Church of Nazarene	Bahai Faith
Congregation of Beth Jacob	Absolute Universal Mind Ministry

The power of prayer: Forty-three percent of Californians say that they pray every day.

How They Traveled

With difficulty!

What they didn't do was pick up the phone to make reservations—and they brought a lot more with them than just one suitcase. Moving west by land or sea, from another continent or another state, is a trial that we moderns have difficulty really imagining. The move west became a bit more convenient after the transcontinental railroad was completed, but it wasn't globetrotting as we know it today.

Whatever opportunities the travelers were seeking—land, gold, or something in-between—geographically California was just plain difficult to reach. A strip of land between the Pacific Ocean and the Sierra Nevada, California was once considered an island.

Moving west by land required leaving on the journey in early spring so the wayfarers would have enough time to plant and harvest food in order to survive during the winter. Their anticipation was much more fundamental and difficult than we would even stop to consider today. And ships that relied on wind were, like the wind, unpredictable and sometimes slow. Today we anticipate travel inconveniences, like lack of legroom and tasteless airline food, with agony. But plant it, hope it grows, and prepare it on the move? I'll have the chicken, please.

★ ★ ★

Wagons rocked and swayed up the Platte Valley land trails. Heavy rains made living muddy and messy but assured plenty of grass for the livestock, which always traveled alongside. Wagon wheels often got stuck in the mud.

A stagecoach notice: "If the team runs away, sit still and take your chances. If you jump, nine times out of ten you will get hurt. Don't swear and lop over on neighbors when sleeping. Never shoot on the road as the noise might frighten the horses."

What do Donner Pass, Peter Lassen's Trail, and Carson's Pass all have in common? They were are all difficult and dangerous routes across the Sierras.

Mrs. Biddy Mason, as part of her master's caravan, trudged from Mississippi to California along with three hundred wagons. Part of her job was to keep the cattle together across the prairies. Years later she and her three daughters won their freedom in California. Due to hard work and clever investments, Mrs. Mason acquired large parcels of land, which she later donated for churches, nursing homes, and schools.

Every pound of freight and every single passenger traveling toward the mines by sea had to pass through the Golden Gate!

All that moving made everyone hungry, and some enterprising people stopped in their tracks and went to work right on the spot. One woman earned $18,000 baking pies in an iron skillet over open campfires to hundreds of hopefuls passing by. George Briggs planted watermelons on twenty-five acres of Sacramento Valley land. He sold $17,000 dollars worth of fruit. Watermelons and pies or burger and fries?

John Butterfield, one of the founders of American Express, was hired to make two trips per week carrying mail from St. Louis and Memphis to San Francisco. His stagecoaches were contracted to travel by way of Arkansas, El Paso, Tucson, Los Angeles, and Fort Smith. Years later he sold his stage line to Wells Fargo.

The Pony Express began in 1860 as a means of carrying mail. Two African American men rode the mail from Stockton to the mines. One of them, George Monroe, became a famous stage driver when he was chosen to drive President Ulysses S. Grant along the curves leading into the Yosemite Valley. Monroe Meadows in Yosimite is named after him. A few years later, Western Union was up and running, putting the Pony Express out of business.

Theodore Dehone Judah, locating engineer for the twenty-two-mile-long Sacramento Railroad, hurried east, urging the development of more railroads in the west. A few years later he shifted his efforts to Sacramento, where a handful of merchants later became known as The Big Four. These big fellows (who were not yet big) were Mark Hopkins, Collis P. Huntington, Charles Crocker, and Leland Stanford. Nor were the Big Four rich—yet. After their initial outlay of only $1,500 each, the Central Pacific Railroad was formed and in 1869 it was completed, making the state vastly more accessible, and the Big Four rich.

San Francisco's population jumped from 57,000 to 234,000 in ten years, making California's population more than Oregon's and Washington's combined. As a whole, the United States population rose 26 percent while California's increased by 47 percent.

Mining experts report that 90 percent of California's gold has yet to be discovered!

Naming Our Towns

Towns are named for any number of reasons in any number of ways. They are a part of our heritage and reflect a connection to our history with the people who traveled before us. Names suggest what those people came across and what they left behind as well as the psychology of the times.

The majority of county names, as well as city and town names, are of Indian and European (Spanish) influence, which we will see soon. But for now, here is a look at a few of our more picturesque town names of English origin.

Orange is in Orange County, and both the city and the county were named after, you guessed it, the fruit.

Peanut [Trinity]. So named in 1900 by the postmaster of Weaverville because the name was unique and because he was fond of peanuts.

Several places have been named after a favorite in the nut family: Walnut. Among them are Walnut Grove in Sacramento County, Walnut Creek in Contra Costa County, and Walnut (changed from Lemon in 1912) in Los Angeles County.

Pudding Creek is derived from the mispronunciation of the words "Put in Creek."

Speaking of mispronunciations, in Napa County, Calistoga was originally supposed to be Saratoga of California. Sam Brannan— the guy who shouted: "gold, Gold, GOLD! In the American River!"—developed the place as a resort, saying he would make it the "Saratoga of California," but he got tongue-tied and it wound up Calistoga.

Rough and Ready was President Zachary Taylor's nickname and was also the name of a town in Nevada County. At one time, there were many places called Rough and Ready, but this is the only mining town from the gold rush days that survives with the same name today.

I'T'S NOT SURPRISING THAT NATIVE AMERICAN names are all over our maps. Tribal names, or words from native languages, are scattered across California, as they are across the country. Here are a few county names:

Colusa, the name comes from the Ko-ru-si Indians. **Inyo,** means "dwelling place of a great spirit." **Modoc,** "People of the south," probably given by their kin to the north, the Klamath Indians. **Mono,** from the Shoshonean Indian term "Monache," a name applied to those Shoshones living east of the Sierra and north of Owens Lake. **Napa,** named after a tribe of Indians said to be the bravest of all the California Indians. **Siskiyou,** meant "bobtailed horse" in the Cree Indian language. **Solano,** named after the great Indian chief. **Tuolumne,** a corruption of the Indian word talma-lamne meaning "a group of stone huts or caves." **Yolo,** the name of a tribe of Patwin Indians, which is said to mean "a place abounding in rushes." **Yuba,** possibly from Yu-ba, which was an ancestral village of Maidu Indians.

SETTLING IN

PEOPLE TRAVELED TO CALIFORNIA to make their fortune or begin a new life on new land.

If they were able to survive actually traveling to it, settling on that land was equally as difficult. Our pioneers weren't calling contractors and builders—that would have required a telephone. They weren't driving all over town to pick up what they needed—that would have required a car and a town. With the abundance and conveniences that we live with today, most of us cannot know how difficult it surely must have been. The hardships they endured were physical, mental, and emotional.

Houses were made of logs. Shelves were built by boring holes into those logs and then by putting in long, strong wooden pins to hold up "shakes" (shingles) of oak.

While their new homes were under construction, women cooked out-doors by building a crossbar in a pit. This allowed them to hang kettles and keep food and water warm. If a prairie wind swept by while they were out cooking, the hems of their long dresses could catch on fire and, thus, bloomers became the style of dress for women of the West. Bloom-ers, by the way, were looked upon with shock, disapproval, and disgust by those who didn't understand that dresses were a fire hazard. Bloomers were not a feminist fashion statement, rather they were a necessity.

Before Dad was able to make a door, Mom hung a blanket in its place. She kept it down with rocks or trunks. Traveling trunks were wooden boxes opened with saws and hammers.

Temporary beds were made of the smoothest surface of a board that was nailed to four posts. One pillow, sometimes made of moss, was a luxury. Moss was also used to stop up the openings between uneven boards while a roof was being built. Bedbugs were common—and annoying, I should think.

Before a well was dug and a pipe was laid, the convenience of water depended on the nearness of the closest running stream. Washing clothes was done by filling buckets, two at a time, and lugging them back to the big metal pot hanging over the big roaring fire. Whether or not the water would boil depended on which way the wind blew. Once the water boiled, the clothes were cleaned with handmade soap, pulled out of the pot with a stick, then hung to dry. In those days, white didn't stay that way for long.

Once a house was built, a closet with a chamber pot was used for a toilet. It had to be emptied outdoors as the odor became very disagreeable very quickly.

Cooking became easier when those who had traveled with ovens and stoves were able to set them up indoors. Vegetables were planted and harvested, cows and chickens provided milk and eggs, pigs provided pork. If the settlers had neighbors, they traded animals and exchanged produce.

The Whisper of a Ghost

WITH THE FEVERISH PITCH the times took on, it didn't take long until the diggin's ran dry.

Why, some ol' timers claim California has never gotten over the effects of the gold rush.

Just the other night, when it was late, I was sitting outside looking at the moon and listening to a cricket chirp. I got to wondering what one of those pioneers might have to say if he could sit down right next to me and strike up a conversation. With a faraway glance to a time long ago, I thought I heard the whisper of a ghost from those great pioneering days of yore:

Heck, it's not so different today. Why, take a look around you. Everywhere you look there's something shining gold. What a climate! Seems like the sun's still shining practically all year long.

There's nothing quite so pretty as the Sierra Nevada, at just a certain time of day, when the setting sun casts a golden glow all across the range. Except for all those yellow poppies and flowers in the fields. Makes them look like slow-moving butterflies dancing across the hills when the wind blows just the right way. Seems like even the sandy desert sparkles yellow flakes as it stretches out to the golden shores of the shining sea.

If you listen closely, you can still hear the voices of the night—it's just mixed up a little different, that's all. The crickets are still chirping, the doves they're still cooing, and the frogs are croaking, same as they used to. There's a train passing by somewhere out there in the night—and a coyote howling, further off even still. It's all still there.

Gold rush saw some good times and some bad times but in a way, it looks like times are repeating themselves. Look at all those pioneers out there in that Silicon Valley. It's the Wild West all over again, 'cept it's the Information Age! And what about all those shining stars out Hollywood way?

There will always be new territory to explore and dreams to be pursued. For all us pioneers of yesteryear, and for you newcomers too, the Golden State continues to shine bright enough to see everybody's dreams come true.

Where We Live

THERE'S ALWAYS SOMETHING GOING ON HERE—boring, California isn't. Our state is always making the news, sometimes it's really good and sometimes it's really bad. When you stop and think about it for a minute, it's not surprising—we seem to come by it naturally. California is a state of extremes. And, since we humans are creatures of the earth and California's location on that earth is extreme, so, it seems, are her people and the things that happen here.

Situated along the continent's western rim, at the farthest edge of the New World, we are just plain far away. WAY out west! Any further and you're swimming in the Pacific Ocean. So, from that standpoint alone, California is remarkable. But in addition to our extreme location, this little strip of land we call home holds within it the most extreme environment of anywhere else on the planet!

Just taking a look at our borders indicates why our environment is incomparable. In simple terms, the state is shaped like an oblong box. The length of one side is 1,264 miles of wild Pacific Coast with Mexico closing it up at one end and Oregon closing it up at the other, while the length of the other side is half rugged mountain range and half scorching, flat desert. Add to that the most fearsome earthquake fault of all, a six-hundred-mile crease through the landscape we call the San Andreas. Then throw into the mix the largest central valley of its kind in the world. As if that's not extreme enough, these boundaries hold within them both the highest (Mt. Whitney) and lowest (Death Valley) points in the continental U.S., and these points are within one hundred miles of each other!

As you can imagine, the weather going on in our state, from one end to the other, is extreme as well. Some parts of the state enjoy all four seasons and others, basically two. The different feel and smells that the seasons bring mean different things to people residing in different parts of the state. Up in coastal Northern California, the Fourth of July may mean bundling up in a sweater and keeping busy, whereas in the deserts or valleys of the South, the sun can be fatal and people stay inside with their air-conditioners running or remain very, very still.

With all this diversity of terrain and climate is it any wonder that our people are equally diverse? The rhythm and style of life is always affected by what the land provides. For example, the way of life at the beach is different than the way of life in the mountains. And city life, depending on the weather, can vary from one city to another. The weather demands that this is so.

The Central Valley, a plain 75 miles wide and 430 miles long, has become the richest farming region in the world. For over fifty years, California has been the nation's number one agriculture state and is now the number one dairy state as well. This one state grows over half of the fruits, nuts, and vegetables that feed all fifty states. In 1997 that weighed out to 39 million tons.

Our location in the world provides us with one other priceless source: the sun. We get plenty of it. With sun and fertile soil, California truly is "the Land of Plenty."

I think it's pretty safe to say that we are the lucky ones who get to call California "home." This state is undeniably rare and remarkable—a place where the land is as unpredictable as the people who live on it. One thing is certain; the possibilities here are endless. If it hasn't already happened, it probably will.

WHERE IN THE WORLD

CALIFORNIA, THE PLACE, and where it is located, is an altogether different matter to a Californian than it is to the rest of the world. California, the place, to someone who does not call California home, is a state of mind. Our place on the map, like our place in the imagination, began hundreds of years ago.

"I'm from California" is a statement that is commonly met with an awestruck look. In the minds of many people we represent a dream—an expectation of something curious and remarkable located out at the furthest edge of the New World where the sun always shines and anything is possible. Those of us who live here are aware of this type of advance billing, but what of the actual location of our state?

California is part of the North American continent, unfolding along its westernmost rim. The San Andreas Fault keeps this state, like its people, moving and shaking—always making news and making noise.

★　★　★

Talk about high pressure! This is where it starts:

California's fault systems are created by the motion of the Pacific and North American plates as they slide past each other at an average speed of two inches per year. Sometimes if rigid material, like granite, impedes the slide, pressure increases as the plates strain to move. When the material gives way, the pent-up pressure is released in a sudden lurch, causing the earth along the fault to quake, tremble, and shudder. I can relate.

The costliest natural disaster in U.S. history, to the tune of $20 billion in damages, was due to an earthquake—and not very long ago at that. On January 17, 1994, in Northridge, Los Angeles County, the ground shook the Richter scale to 6.7. The city of Fillmore in Ventura county was moved west by two inches.

The World Series was postponed due to an earthquake in 1989. The second game of the series between two California teams, the San Francisco Giants and the Oakland Athletics, was about to begin when tremors in the Bay Area sent the Richter Scale to 7.1 and fans screaming.

San Francisco, 1906. With its epicenter in Marin County, a deadly earthquake broke gas and water mains. The fires that followed destroyed much of San Francisco. In those days, rumors took the place of mass media. Some were that Vesuvius had erupted, San Diego's Hotel del Coronado had fallen into the sea, and coast cities had been deluged by a tidal wave.

Of a sudden we had found ourselves staggering and reeling . . . sickening swaying of the earth . . . a great cornice crushed a man as if he were a maggot. . . .

P. BARRETT, *San Francisco Examiner*
April 19, 1906

Kodak's Brownie Camera. This camera was the reason for the existence of so many views of the 1906 San Francisco quake-fire. It was the first camera that could be loaded during the day and on the spot. In 1895, the camera sold for $5.00.

Since the San Francisco quake in 1906, the next biggest fault rupture was in Landers, San Bernardino. Ground shifts of fifteen to twenty feet were measured.

Of the thirteen major earthquakes in California, all but two have occurred in the morning, between approximately 2:30 and 10:30.

Reports from Caltech say that from 1987 to 1994, Southern California had over 121,000 minor quakes.

Weather or Not

Because of where we are located in the world, we have the most diverse environment on the planet, which is really saying something. This means, naturally, that California has diverse weather, as well. For example, it is not uncommon that a twenty-minute drive can see a fifteen-degree temperature change. Air conditioners and heaters are turned on and off as often as the sweaters we change in and out of.

Like the environment and the state itself, our weather can be dramatic. California can experience dense fog, heat waves that commonly claim lives, dry Santa Ana winds that blow fire, and torrential downpours that flood—all in the same day.

Anywhere one lives, weather defines the rhythm of life. Although not all of California enjoys sunshine all year around, the rest of world seems to think we do. Why, the very mention of the word "California" brings about longing sighs, dreamy eyes, and comments like, "You're so lucky—all that glorious sunshine." And compared to most places we do, indeed, enjoy a wonderful climate. There is no doubt that, because of our location, we can boast of weather that so many elsewhere desire. Of all our ample resources, the sun is California's leading resource. For health, pleasure, psychology, real estate, agriculture, and recreation, sunshine affects just about everything it touches. It is only one of the many reasons our population doubles every eighteen years.

The sunshine of the Golden State—it is the stuff of legends and dreams.

There is a lot to be said for consistency, well, because it is reliable. Some 80 percent of the state's thirty-two and a half million inhabitants reside within a band of land forty miles wide between Santa Rosa (approximately fifty miles north of the Bay area) south to San Diego, where from May to November weather is consistently clear and, on the average, 72 degrees.

Early filmmakers came to Southern California for the light—some areas offer over three hundred clear-sky days a year—along with diverse terrain, making location and outdoor shooting ideal.

If you want to steer clear of rain, Bagdad, in San Bernardino County, may be your place. The longest rainless period in U.S. history lasted there for 993 days, from 1909 to 1912.

All that sun dries out the vegetation, and fires are common when dry Santa Ana winds fuel them fiercely. To those familiar with the Santa Ana winds, their distinct smell and feel make them predictable before they actually blow into town. At up to one hundred miles an hour, the dry winds blow out of the hot deserts of Southern California. They often blow in around Halloween, bringing fire, and can be spooky.

And for those who prefer the drama and beauty of contrast, California offers that too:

In parts of Berkeley, it is said that the fog drip alone is equivalent to ten inches of rain a year.

It was Mark Twain who said, "The coldest winter I ever spent was a summer in San Francisco."

Summer in the Mojave Desert is a flat, dry, fire zone where mangled cactus, called Joshua trees, reach twisted and gnarled arms out of the sun-raped earth. Joshua trees do not grow anywhere in the world except for the Mojave Desert. What an eerie and spectacular sight they are. The Mormon pioneers are said to have named them after the prophet Joshua, from the Old Testament, because the trees seemed to be waving to them with upraised arms—on toward the promised land.

In the summer, Point Reyes is the coolest place in the continental U.S.

How's this for a contrast? Mt. Whitney, the highest point in the continental U.S. at 14,495 feet and snow-peaked year-round, is only one hundred miles away from the lowest point of land in the Western Hemisphere, Death Valley, which sits 282 feel below sea level, where summer temperatures consistently reach over 120 degrees F.

In one year, 1986, thirty-four counties in Northern California experienced floods.

Days you do not want to be camping: The most rain to fall in one minute occurred at Opids Camp, Los Angeles—0.65 of an inch. The most rain to fall in one hour occurred in Monterey, where the sky dumped 5.75 inches. The most rain to fall in twenty-four hours was 26.12 inches at Hoegees Camp in Los Angeles.

The most snow to fall in one day was sixty-seven inches in 1982 at Echo Summit in El Dorado County. California's snowiest year was 1911. The most snow to fall in the entire nation occurred that year in January at the appropriately named Alpine County, the same place and year that experienced the greatest snow depth in the entire nation: 451 inches.

The national record for wind duration was set at Point Reyes: 365 days a year, twenty-four hours a day, at twenty-three miles an hour. The speediest wind occurred in Monterey, in 1950, clocking in at 115 MPH.

Nevada County holds the record for the coldest temperature in state history for forty-five degrees below zero on January 20, 1937, at Boca. The hottest temperature fried Death Valley on July 10, 1913, when the mercury rose—to 134 degrees!

Lightning in Trinity County once struck 150 times in a five-mile area.

Do you know what created the Salton Sea? A natural flood occurring in 1905 was exacerbated by man-made diversions of the Colorado River causing two years of flooding that resulted in forming the Salton Sea.

Sometimes a pyramid-shaped fog bank, one hundred times larger than Cheops, forms over Richardson Bay in Marin County.

Where sunscreen sales are high: In parts of Riverside and San Bernardino counties, the sun shines more than three hundred days a year.

Well, it is established, California experiences a diversity of climate. But whether we like it or not, and most of us do, part of what makes this state so special is the overall mild climate and our fabulous sunshine. So much so that our legendary weather is, in part, the reason we are known around the world as Eden, The Land of the Sundown Sea, The New Greece, The American Italy, and Pacific Eden.

SHAKING ALL AROUND

At approximately 7:30 A.M. on October 17, 1987, I was setting about the task of getting myself and my fifth-grade classroom at Sunrise Elementary School in East Los Angeles ready for another day. What I could not know was that this would be no ordinary day. By 7:42 A.M., an earthquake of significant magnitude began.

Although severe jolting movement should have inspired me to run for cover, it didn't. Instead, I stood in front of a cabinet that was propelling pencils, markers, and construction paper. Impressed that the entire building had been lifted up off the ground, I thought, "If Godzilla were real, this is what it would feel like if he picked up the earth and shook it like some kind of play toy."

The second temblor arrived shortly thereafter. This time I decided to do the sensible thing and get out of the room. Truth told, we natives know what we're supposed to do; after all, we were weaned on earth movements. We're supposed to duck and cover under a desk or stand in a doorway. So I dispensed with the theoretical and moved into practical mode, thinking, "I don't want to be trapped in this building alone!"

Many students and most of the faculty arrive at school early, so when I stepped out onto the playground, I saw each and every person on campus in a drop position on the field. This was the first earthquake for most of my students and for many of the faculty as well. Consequently, the calming presence they tried to provide was, well, shall we say, not very effective.

I searched my mind for calming things to do. For some reason, I thought of doing the dance called the "Hokey Pokey." It might

just provide distraction to the alternately terrified, distraught, and otherwise delirious student population this day. The shaking stopped. I called to the children who were standing in straight lines trying to fight back their tears. I asked them to come and form a circle around me.

It turned out, ironically, that doing the "Hokey Pokey" really saved the day! "You put your right foot in, you put your right foot out, you put your right foot in and you shake it all about." And shake we do, here in California.

SUSAN TENENBAUM, Burbank

H₂O

No two ways about it, water in this state is a constant problem and a matter of dispute.

About seventy-five percent of the state's demand for water comes from south of Sacramento, while about seventy-five percent of the state's precipitation falls north of Sacramento. Problem. Those who have water fight with those who want it. To compensate, California has developed elaborate water storage and transportation systems.

Major urban water systems began in 1913 when the Los Angeles Aqueduct opened. Beginning in 1929, Oakland and other East Bay cities received water via the Mokelumne Aqueduct from water that the Sierra Nevada provided. The Sierra Nevada/Central Valley river system began in the 1930s with the Central Valley Project, which included huge structures like Shasta Dam. San Francisco, in 1934, began to receive water from Yosemite National Park through the Hetch Hetchy Aqueduct. In 1941, the Colorado Aqueduct opened, carrying water from Lake Havasu to the San Diego border. The State Water Project (via the California Aqueduct) began to get water to Southern California in 1972 from Oroville Reservoir in the Sacramento Valley. There, water is diverted from the Colorado River and pumped over the Tehachapi Mountains.

Tremendous amounts of water are moved from hundreds of miles away through the state by a complex system that involves dams, aqueducts, hundreds of miles of irrigation canals, siphons, pumps, bays, weirs, and drains. Without this massive transport of water, the immense thirst of California would not be quenched and agriculture would not be possible.

Even so, the water on which much of the state does rely is not great. It often contains impurities, even with a filter. Walking around with a designer water bottle is not as pretentious as a nonlocal might assume.

"Water is life. Don't waste it."

YOSEMITE VALLEY

On Merced River near Snelling
Merced Co., Cal., July 14th [1868].

Dear Bro. David,

*I have lived under the sunny sky of California near 3½ months,
but have not yet rec'd a single letter from any source—perhaps a
few went to the dead letter off[ice] while I was in the mountains,
but I am settled now with a ranchman for eight or nine months
and hope to enjoy a full share of the comfort of letters during my
long isolation.*

*I traveled along the San Jose Valley from San Fran. to Gilroy and
crossed the Diablo Mountains by the Pacheco Pass, crossed the
plains and river of the San Joaquin, and traveled on into the Sierra
Nevadas to the mammoth trees and magnificent Yo Semite Valley,
thence down the Merced to this place.*

*My health, which suffered such a wreck in the South, has been
thoroughly patched and mended in the mountains of California . . .
a month in the Sierra cooled with mountain winds and delicious
crystal water has effected a complete cure.*

*And now Davie, this is splendid country, and one might truthfully
make use of more than half of the Methodist hymn "Land of pure
delight" in describing it, and it flows with more of milk and more
of honey than ever did old Canaan in its happiest prime. Of all the
bright shining ranks of happy days that God has given me since I
left Wisconsin, these of California are the happiest.*

Affectionately,
J.M. [John Muir]

MAGNIFICENT

I grew up in Granada Hills, a city in the San Fernando Valley, where it seemed like every day was hot and dry. I was in for a big change when I arrived in Arcata, a logging town near Eureka, to begin college at Humboldt State. It was 800 miles away from home and two hours away from the Oregon border. My room-mate was a girl from Los Gatos named Mary Hill. Our dorms were situated in a canyon that hugged the bosom of a mountain valley where the smell of pulp and sounds of nature got trapped, something neither of us was used to. I remember one stormy night it just rained so hard that a waterfall formed in the canyon just across from our room. Mary was so impressed by the sight and sound of it that she felt the need to make a loud statement at 2:00 A.M. She woke me up by dramatically flinging open our curtains to nature's stage and shouted, "Isn't it magnificent!?" And I had to agree, it was.

ESTHER FLINK, Granada Hills

Names the Europeans Left Behind

It's interesting and fun to discover from where names come. The Native Americans were here long before the first Europeans arrived. How long? About twelve thousand years. Which Europeans? It's pretty easy to deduce when you take a look at thirty-one of our fifty-eight county names, ten of which either begin with San or Santa. Here is a look at most (sorry, I can't fit them all) of the county names the Spanish left behind:

Alameda County
Alameda means "road lined with trees." The county seat is Oakland.

Calaveras County
Means "exposed skulls," which were found along the river banks. The county seat is San Andreas, which was named by Mexican miners in 1848.

Del Norte County
This is the most "of the north" county in the state. The county seat is Orleans Bar.

El Dorado County
"The Land of the Gilded Man," so named because gold was discovered there. The county seat is Placerville.

Fresno County
"Ash tree." The county seat is also Fresno.

Los Angeles County
Meaning "the angels," the name is used both for the county and the county seat.

Mariposa County

Mariposa means "butterfly." The county seat, another butterfly.

Merced County

The county name means "mercy," where the county seat is more of the same.

Monterey County

"Hill of the king," where he sits is in Salinas, the county seat.

Nevada County

What do Nevada and Sierra County have in common? They are both up north, sit along the Sierra Nevada Mountain Range, and indicate COLD. Nevada means "snow covered" and Sierra means "saw-toothed." Nevada's county seat is Nevada City. The county seat of Sierra is the old boomtown of Downieville.

Sacramento County

Named in honor of the Holy Sacrament, the name Sacramento receives a triple honor: county name, county seat, and state capital.

Land of Plenty

When people think of California they don't usually associate it with farming or agriculture. The fact is, however, we have so much of it that, in true California style, we have given it a special name—"Agribusiness." And it's big. Our Great Central Valley, also known as the "state's heartland," a plain 75 miles wide and some 430 miles long, has become the richest farming region in the history of the world!

California produces 350 different crops and commodities including oil, cotton, dairy, livestock, and fruits and vegetables such as apples, strawberries, avocados, olives, grapes, sugar beets, lettuce, nuts, potatoes, alfalfa, tomatoes, watermelon, and pumpkin. Organic and nonorganic, the grocery list continues to unfold long enough to fulfill any gourmet's dream.

And what about all that sun-kissed citrus growing in our Inland Empire? Setting up a lemonade stand is still an easy way for young children to take that first step toward independence. Citrus, golden fruits of California, grown by golden sun, here in our Land of Plenty: the Golden State.

★   ★   ★

Richard Smoley, the editor of *California Farmer,* says: "Each farmer feeds eighty-two people. Americans eat better than citizens of any other nation and pay less."

The top ten agricultural counties are: Fresno, Tulare, Monterey,

Kern, Merced, San Joaquin, Stanislaus, San Diego, Riverside, and Imperial. In 1997, for the first time in California history, each produced at least $1 billion of agricultural goods. Wow!

By the 1980s, California had the dubious distinction of being the nation's leading producer of marijuana.

More cotton is grown in Kern County than in the rest of the U.S.

Modoc County is the cowboy corner of California. Cattle ranching has been its agricultural mainstay since the first ranchers arrived in the area in the 1860s.

Because we had developed rice growing and processing to such an art, the Chinese government sent two experts to California for advice during the late 1940s. Fall River Valley in Shasta County produces twenty-five percent of the wild rice marketed in the entire world.

Gridley in Butte County is the kiwi capitol of the U.S.

Agostin Haraszthy, a nobleman and army officer banished from his homeland of Hungary, traveled to California in search of the perfect place to plant vineyards. Impressed by the climate in Sonoma Valley, Haraszthy traveled back to Europe and then returned to California with a hundred thousand cuttings of three hundred varieties of grapes, which were planted all over the state. He produced a Zinfandel that was California's first world-famous wine and wrote a book titled *Grape Culture, Wines, and Winemaking,* which became the winemakers' bible of its era.

Charles Krug, Paul Masson, Almaden, Martini and Mondavi, Guasti, Inglenook, and Asti. Italian, French, and Swiss immigrants came to the cities of Napa, Fresno, Modesto, Madera, Cucamonga, as well as the Sonoma, San Joaquin, and Sacramento valleys to establish wineries, many of which have become internationally important.

The Groves family produces notable wines from an unlikely place, the Trinity Lake region. Alpen Cellars is a family-owned business whose members are responsible for every aspect of the work that goes into running it. They have been known to prune the fall crush on snowshoes.

Ah, the nectar of the gods. The United States is the fifth leading producer of wine in the world. California is responsible for 92 percent of U.S. wine.

Speaking of wine as the nectar of the gods, apparently it is the nectar of plenty of mortals too. Check out these great grape numbers! By 1985, revenue produced from grapes alone totaled $292.1 in Fresno County, $152.7 in Kern County, and Tulare County contributed $194.8 million. Once known as agriculture, farmers, and farms, in California we give special businesses special names. Today they are known as agribusiness, growers, and ranches—and how grateful we are to all of them, whether big or small.

Another popular drink in California—milk. We produce more milk and cheese than any other U.S state, having surpassed Wisconsin in 1993, which had been the leader since 1915.

One Holstein-Friesian cow, belonging to Manuel Maciel & Son of Hanford, set the record for yielding 465,224 pounds of milk in twenty years of her busy life.

Menu from 1918:

Soup	$	.01
Salad		.01
Coffee		.01
Steak		.75
TOTAL	$	.78
(No tax!)		

What do you get when you cross Walter Knott and Rudolph Boysen? Knott's Berry Farm! Walter Knott, a berry farmer, and his wife, Cordelia, set up a berry stand on a dusty road in San Luis Obispo in 1920. Times were tough. When Walter's cousin offered him a partnership on twenty acres in Buena Park, the Knotts moved to Orange County, where they set up a bigger roadside stand and Cordelia started baking pies and canning jams. Walter learned of a bigger, better berry that Rudolph Boysen of Anaheim was developing. When Knott and Boysen crossed paths and berries, their business boomed. Motorists jammed Cordelia's tearoom, waiting for her berry pie made of her newest menu addition, chicken dinners with biscuits and gravy. To entertain his waiting patrons, Walter set up a Wild West town by dismantling buildings from an abandoned mining town in Arizona. These "seeds" blossomed into the world's first theme park: Knott's Berry Farm.

Indio is the nation's largest date shipper. The fruit, I mean.

Gilroy is the nation's top garlic producer and harvests fifty million pounds per year.

It is possible for a single prune tree to produce a half ton of prunes per year.

The oldest, tallest, and largest redwood trees are California grown. Many of the Victorian mansions in Northern California were made possible because of the timber bounty, especially redwood. Of the ten leading lumber-producing states, California is second. Of course, you know that the redwood is the official state tree.

Westwood in Lassen County was the home of Red River Lumber Company that operated from 1913 to 1956. They were the largest pine lumber mill in the world. Breathe deep and imagine the smell.

Cannery Row in Monterey began as a Chinese immigrant fishing community in the 1850s. The early explorers told fish tales of sardines, salmon, and sturgeon so numerous that they could practically be scooped up out of the bays and streams. The golden trout is the state fish. You knew that too, right?

Of all the western states, California leads in the production of catfish. Aquaculturalists produced $9 million worth in 1994—and over $5 million each in sales for bass, abalone, and algae.

The Coleman National Fish Hatchery (north of Red Bluff) in Tehama County rears thirteen to fifteen million chinook salmon and one million steelhead annually.

While gold was discovered in Northern California, black gold was discovered in Southern California. Oil was the lifeblood that sustained the growth in Orange County at the turn of the century. Union, Standard, and Chevron discovered and drilled oil in many Orange County towns such as Fullerton, Brea, Anaheim, Huntington Beach, Placentia, and La Habra. Today, Kern County in the southern Central Valley produces more oil than some OPEC countries!

An oil derrick sits on the track and field area of Beverly Hills High School. Can you stand it?

Location, location, location. The fifty-six-acre Fujishige strawberry farm is the last undeveloped lot in the resort district of Anaheim, sitting right next door to Disneyland. Two brothers, Hiroshi and Maseo Fujishige, sons of Japanese immigrant farmers, purchased the land in 1954 and have steadfastly refused offers to sell their land—offers that have gone as high as $32 million. They prefer to get up at 3:00 every morning simply for the love of farming. Disney recently made an offer estimated between $70 and 90 million for 52.5 acres, which the Fujishiges are considering. Part of the deal? The family insists on keeping the remaining 3.5 acres.

In Corning, Tehama County, the two-olive martini is not a problem. Corning is the olive capitol of the U.S.

And where do you think the "Raisin Capital of the World" might be? That's right—Selma, Fresno County. Ninety-five percent of raisins grown in the U.S. are within a forty-mile radius of the town.

Ninety-nine to 100 percent of United States' almonds, artichokes, dates, figs, kiwifruit, persimmons, pistachios, raisins, clovers, and walnuts are California grown.

This state leads the nation in seventy-four crop and livestock commodities and rates number one in the United States for net farm income. In 1997, California's cash farm receipts and income totaled a record $26.8 billion. This kind of abundance allows Californians to shop at neighborhood farmers markets all across the state. We can remain health conscious and still experience fine dining. When you mix together all these fabulous ingredients, it's called California cuisine.

THE LANDSCAPE OF HOME

I grew up in the first of a long row of houses, a Southern California suburban neighborhood, the homes situated side by side. What a glorious world my parents provided for my brother, sister, and I; all natives, for we were loved, healthy, and safe.

My childhood was protected by something in addition to my parents—although I didn't realize it at the time. Just on the other side of the brick wall and patch of grass that claimed our backyard as ours was "the orange grove"—just a toss away. Like the home we grew up in, the family who lived there was protected by acres and acres of dense orange groves.

Their blossoms smelled like heaven in the night, yet the groves themselves held within them secret tales of caution and chance that brought dreams of danger and adventure. My walk to school could have been cut in half if only I was allowed to cut through those groves, shrouded by walls of forbidding and imposing eucalyptus trees.

I remember when they chopped the first acre down. The empty space left a wide open spot in the field and along with that the opportunity to actually see into the grove. In a far corner, my mother, sister, and I discovered a big, two-story, abandoned, and ancient-looking house. It must have been two hundred years old. We all looked into each other's eyes, not daring to speak the question we all asked in our minds.

The freshly plowed earth was still damp and cloying with the pungency of fresh and rotting oranges, shaken from the overturned trees. As we tiptoed across the forbidden land, I glanced over my shoulder, afraid of being caught by someone or something deeper in the quiet grove, which had now completely absorbed the sounds of suburbia beyond it.

Cautiously we approached the house. At the bottom of the long and splintered steps, we hesitated, then we creaked one-by-one up the stairs until we reached the top. We turned the rusted, iron doorknob that hung from the heavy door and tentatively swung the door open, wondering who and what we might find inside. We three stood there, side by side, and looked up high to the end of the wooden staircase. It rose cathedral-like to a broken window, where beams of sunlight caught the dust our feet had stirred in its rays of white light.

Our exploration continued upstairs, where our next discovery bedazzled my young eyes: treasure chests full of mysterious and fascinating old books that must have been a thousand years old, for they were nothing like I had ever seen before. Strange and indecipherable, some were gold and cracked, dozens were old and tattered, still more were leather bound with yellowed pages. Every one of them held within it a mystery that was heaven to my young imagination, for each was written in scrolls and squiggles foreign to us all. After a long period of silence, my mother deciphered that they were German, and after much scrutiny, we discovered publishing dates back to the early 1800s.

Gradually all the trees were torn up and the groves were replaced with condominiums and strip malls. But by then I was anxious to explore beyond the unspoken boundaries the orange groves had represented in my life, beyond the tales I had grown up with.

The fruit grown within them was precious, and if we, the guardians of the groves, could not trespass in them, nor then could anyone else.

LEZLIE ELIZABETH, Orange

Groves of Gold

What is it about the notion of orange groves—seeing them, smelling them—that can make you feel as if you have just traveled back in history? Simply the advertising imprinted on the side of an old, wooden packing crate can take you back to another place and time. Here you stand in the middle of a grove of oranges edged with swaying palms. Here you are surrounded by long, narrow rows of dark-green leafed and orange-ornamented trees. Here, again, you find yourself in a time of spacious cobalt skies, when sunshine and moonbeams led the way like the yellow brick road to the foothills of the San Bernardino Mountains.

County fairs celebrated the fruit whose juice promoted health and wealth. Greetings from California accompanied crates packed with Cucamonga, Corona Beauty, or Valencia oranges. Whichever variety was chosen, the fruit enticed the recipients with the wonders of the West and also promoted California as a virtual paradise.

What remains today of the Southern California orange industry is concentrated primarily in the Inland Empire of Riverside and San Bernardino counties. But even as far as the coast, at just the right time of spring, the fragrance of orange blossoms intermingles with that of night-blooming jasmine, producing a fragrance as powerful as it is intoxicating and with it a reminder of why California loves romancing the orange.

★　★　★

William Wolfskill, Kentucky born, came to California by way of the Old Spanish Trail to trap otter and trade furs. But in 1841, his brothers—Sarchel, Mathus, Milton, and John Reed—joined William, and they planted orange groves in Yolo and Solano counties.

San Bernardino's ("San Berdoo" to the locals) billion-dollar citrus industry started with six orange trees. Anson Van Leuven brought the trees to the San Bernardino Valley from the San Gabriel Valley in 1857.

One of California's two original navel orange trees grows at the corner of Magnolia and Arlington Avenues in Riverside. In 1873, horticulturist Eliza Tibbets received them from the U.S. Department of Agriculture. By 1910, over one hundred thousand acres across the state were planted with the progeny of her trees.

Citrus was worthy of celebration. The first citrus fair in the world was staged in Riverside in February, 1879.

In 1904, G. Harold Powell was sent to California by the U.S. Department of Agriculture to help the citrus farmers solve the problem of spoilage in long-distance shipping. He became so successful in the industry that within four years "the Powell era" had been launched. Mr. Powell died in Pasadena in 1922 while attending a public dinner.

> *Pasadena is a beautiful place. The mountains are nearby, and the views down the valleys are magnificent. The houses are costly and elegant on some of the streets.*
>
> G. HAROLD POWELL, 1904

The first Orange Show, a celebration of the Inland Empire's produce, was held in 1911 in San Bernardino. The cost to produce that show was $744.25. The receipts collected tallied $1180.25. With a profit of $436.00, the health and financial value of citrus was apparent to promoters. The Orange Show has taken place every year since, with the exception of the World War II years, 1942–46, and is still going strong.

TOP OF THE WORLD

I was born in 1921. When I was growing up almost everyone lived in a house next to, or alongside, an orange grove. For a few days every spring, when the groves had their blossoms in full bloom, the whole town smelled like a huge perfume factory.

As young boys, our holiday favorite was a toss-up either between Christmas or the 4th of July. In about the middle of June every year, my younger brothers and I would go into the nearby orange grove and pick perhaps ten dozen oranges. We then set up a card table at the curbing in front of our house and squeezed orange juice. We sold it to thirsty merchants and neighbors for 5 cents a glass. Usually by the second or third of July, we had a coffee can full of coin. That was how we bought our cherry bombs, radio salutes, and silver-powder firecrackers.

At 6:00 A.M. on the 4th of July, my brothers and I slipped out of our house. In the grove near our home ran a creek with banks perhaps eight feet high. On the south bank, a tall, skinny tree grew to a height of about fifty feet. All of us used to shinny about half way up, at which point we ran out of footholds and branches, so we nailed in wooden, ladder-steps in order to get to the top. At that age, this was an absolute necessity. We wanted our Tarzan yells to be heard clear across town. Once up there, we were amazed that we could see miles and miles of orange trees and in the background, a section of the sparkling Pacific Ocean and Catalina Island.

Since I was the oldest and strongest brother, I had the honor of awakening the neighborhood. I placed the cherry bomb in the leather pocket of my slingshot while one of my brothers lit the fuse. I then shot the cherry bomb as high as possible, probably about three hundred feet, and from out there in the middle of the orange grove, at the top of our world, the official start of the 4th of July had begun.

CLIFFTON THOMAS, JR., Fullerton

SANTA CLARA SUMMER CAMP

I am American, of Mexican descent, first generation, and was born on Friday morning, December 13, 1957. I was number nine in a family of eleven children. There would have been thirteen but two of my siblings died prematurely. So, after being pregnant every year for thirteen years my mother decided to stop, or maybe it was my dad's idea for economic reasons. Either way, this brings me to my early childhood recollections.

I remember being carefully placed up a tree in a prune box by my older brother. The box was about two feet wide, by three feet long, and about eighteen inches deep. Judging by the size of this box, I must have been around sixteen months old—too young to pick prunes in an orchard the size of the entire state of Rhode Island. So there I was, lying in this box, watching my whole family pick prunes and being moved from tree to tree.

As the summers continued, I became an active member in helping my family pick prunes. Later on I found out the reason we picked prunes wasn't because we were poor and needed the money. No, it was because my parents always took us on a shopping spree for new clothes just before school started each year. How else would my father clothe all these children and still provide food and

shelter? Naturally, he put us kids to work. I guess maybe that's why none of us ever became good swimmers—while other kids were at summer camp or junior lifeguard classes, we were out there picking fruit.

As we got older, my brothers and I become more ambitious. We wanted new bikes, toys, and, yes, candy—lots of it! We never had an allowance, so we made up for lost time. We followed the fruit season, just after school let out. Starting with cherries in mid-June, we followed that with apricots in early July. We took a couple of weeks off before prune season, and in August, if we had some extra time, we'd squeeze in pears. On the weekends during October, we'd pick walnuts, but that only lasted two seasons because we enjoyed being in school. We lived in the Santa Clara Valley, and at that time orchards were everywhere. I remember one of my uncles boasting about how San Jose was the "prune capital of the world."

My dad had a regular job in the construction business in Redwood City. It was a forty-minute drive for him on the freeway and in order to get to work on time, we got up every morning at 6:00 A.M. so that he could drop us off in the fields on his way to work. It was luxury if you got to ride up front with my parents. It was still dark. My job was to fill up the five-gallon water container so we would all have something to drink during the day.

During the early part of my career of working in the fields, my family experimented in picking all kinds of fruits and vegetables. We tried picking chilies one season. It was hard work and if you ever had an itch in your eye and you scratched it, you were out for the day; the irritation was unbearable. I mentioned cherries. We gave that up because it took too many cherries to fill a basket.

Pears too. They were too much of a hassle because you had to carry this ring, and the pears could be no smaller than the size of that stupid ring.

The last six seasons before I turned eighteen, we settled on picking apricots in July and prunes in August. The boys did the picking; my mom and sisters sliced them open to prepare them for drying. These two fruits were the most profitable for my family.

Even though it was hard work, I will always cherish those memories of working and playing in the fields. It symbolized what California was all about for me during the '60s and early '70s— the fruit basket to the world.

JERRY MACHADO, Santa Clara

You Take the High Road
and I'll Take the Freeway

For many of us, the take-your-time and do-drop-in days of Route 66 are over. Not that we can't have nostalgia if we so choose. The old roads are still out there and some of them are still marked, but the sleepy towns that scattered dusty roads to service motorists crossing Route 66 are not what they used to be.

Of course there are other methods of getting from here to there, but California has become so congested and well-traveled that people tend to base the very decision on where to live on the access to or distance from a freeway. Just about everybody in California is affected in one way or another by freeways.

Road travel is a big part of the California way of life, whether city or country bound. A magazine writer proposed in 1923 that the state flower in California should be the motor car.

Freeway travel is so common that the signs that mark them have an unconscious effect on us. Usually, we pass under freeway signs without much notice. But have you ever noticed how, after heading out on a trip and sitting back to get comfortable, the free-way signs start to look unfamiliar and you realize you have trav-eled far from home—and then, on the way back, your heart beats a little faster when you again begin to recognize the freeway signs? It's funny how the numbers and colors of freeway signs have become our markers of home.

★　★　★

Interstate highway signs are red, white, and blue. California highway signs are green. And those cool black and white, badge-shaped signs, like the old Route 66 sign, are United States highway signs.

Did you know that the Interstate highways which are EVEN numbered (for example Highway 80) run east and west? Yes, that's right, the ODD numbered (like Highway 5) run north and south.

An oldie but a goodie: The first suspension bridge, Bidwell Canyon Bridge in Butte County, was built in 1856. It was relocated to avoid submergency in Lake Oroville, but it's still in use after 143 years.

A State Bureau of Highways was founded in 1895—for wagons.

Arroyo Seco Parkway, six miles of road that became the Pasadena Freeway, was the first of the superhighways. It had an overpass and other "detailed" construction and was completed in 1940.

The first state toll road, the Foothill Tollway in Orange County, was built in 1993 and cost federal and state taxpayers nothing. On the other hand, Clinton Myers became rich and a hero to commuters in the Los Angeles area when he was awarded a $14.8 million bonus for repairing the earthquake-damaged Santa Monica Freeway. How's this for inspiration? For every day the work was completed ahead of schedule Myers earned $200,000. The project was completed seventy-four days early.

Wherever you go, you're covered. And depending on your navigating skills, the fun or confusing part of highway travel is that in progressive California fashion, many of them cross, blend, and intersect, offering several routes to the same destination.

The state's major highways: Highway 1, a coastal road also known in Southern California as Pacific Coast Highway (PCH), runs from Eureka to San Juan Capistrano. Interstate 5 runs from the Oregon border, through the Central Valley, into Los Angeles and on to the Mexican border. Interstate 10, heads out from Santa Monica, past Riverside, through Indio and Blythe into Arizona. Interstate 15 runs from San Diego, through San Bernardino and Barstow, and into Nevada. Highway 49 meanders from the Yuba Pass through the gold rush country to Mariposa. Interstate 80, glides out of San Francisco, through Sacramento, to Nevada. Highway 99 runs from Red Bluff to the southern end of the Central Valley. Don't forget Highway 101, which runs from the Oregon border, across the Golden Gate, and into Los Angeles. And Highway 395, from Carson City, through Bishop, heads right up to San Bernardino.

You can fill up at any one of California's 8,387 gas stations.

In the greater Los Angeles Basin, there are eight interstate highways, thirty-two state highways, and one U.S. highway, 101, which runs through . . .

San Francisco, where the greater San Francisco area has nine interstates, twenty-one state highways, and the same U.S. highway, 101.

The Golden Gate Bridge is part of highway 101. How much steel wire is in its cables? Enough to circle Earth at the equator three and a half times. Seem excessive? Perhaps, unless you're the one crossing it.

The San Francisco–Oakland Bay Bridge is the most traveled toll bridge in California, seeing a daily average of 254,000 commuters, over twice as many as the first runner-up, the Golden Gate.

In 1899:

WAGON SPOKES	$ .30 − .45
BUGGIES AND ROAD WAGONS	
RE-TIRED	$ 10.00
INSTALLATION OF NEW BRAKES	$ 8.00 − 10.00

What's the fifth worst place in the country to drive? According to one hundred expert drivers and *Popular Mechanics* magazine, the entire Los Angeles freeway system.

The most likely time to be injured in a collision is Friday between 5:00 and 6:00 P.M.

An option remains to freeway driving: walking—and Plennie L. Windo, of Santa Monica, liked to do it backwards. At eighty-one years old, Windo walked backward from Santa Monica to San Francisco—in eighty-five days.

The Ronald Reagan Freeway is in Ventura County.

Our freeways are equipped with approximately thirteen thousand call boxes for roadside emergencies from which the CHP receives over three thousand calls a day.

In 1905, in Sacramento County, there were 27 automobiles registered. Five years later there were seven-hundred.

Today, there are over twenty million licensed drivers in California and thirty-five million vehicles that travel 271 billion miles each year.

Odd Facts and Questions

What is so long it would reach from Charleston, South Carolina, to Boston, Massachusetts? California's shoreline.

Who is the average Californian? A thirty-two-year-old white or Latino female, living in the Los Angeles Basin.

Standard Oil removed over one thousand billboards in 1924 from the highways because "they detracted from the natural beauty of the roads."

California is bigger than eighty-five of the smallest nations in the world put together.

How did night driving first become safe? By attaching an electric light to a horse's forehead. That happened first in 1883 in Napa County.

The richest Native Americans in the United States are 172 Aguas Calientes who own 31,000 acres of Palm Springs land.

The word "oak" appears in 150 California place names.

Our Work Ethic

THE CALIFORNIA WORK ETHIC dates back to the dreams and desires of the daring pioneers. Even with the luxuries of modern transportation, California is still a state that is considered far away; it takes a long time to travel this far west. We can be certain that for the settlers, whether braving the high seas or crossing the nearly impassable Sierra Nevada Mountain Range, their trips were grim and grueling. They could only bring with them what they could carry, expecting to create what they needed from what resources they found. The first pioneers to arrive found a lot of sun and fertile soil—but not much else. They could have turned back, but they didn't. The people that sought to call California home were those of a true pioneering spirit, risk takers who knew no bounds and dared to dream of a new freedom and better life in this difficult to reach, daunting, and untamed territory.

The gold rush sparked the biggest mass migration in the history of the world. Thirty-two and a half million people now reside in California making this the most populated state in all the United States, which is the third most-populated country in the world. Among us there are, and have been, inventors, scientists, entrepreneurs, Nobel laureates, and U.S. presidents. Whether a CEO or punching a time clock, our people have bravely pushed forward, daring to make a difference and to go places that had previously been unfashionable or unfathomable to go. California is the home of the brave, a modern place that often sets a pace ahead of tradition. We are a progressive, determined, and hardworking people who have all contributed to making California the state of golden promise, where even the sky is not a limit.

The allure that brought people to California yesterday is the same allure that brings people to California today. Just as some of the first settlers came to California with only a conviction to invent what they needed to make their dreams come true, progressive people continue to come to California with nothing more than their ideas and their dreams. Visionists then, visionists now, this is a state where imagination is queen and invention is king. For many of us, this propensity for hard work and progressive thinking is all we have ever known.

We are the people of a state that makes things happen in an unparalleled fashion. Our trillion-dollar economy is one of the largest and most diverse on the planet. Within the boundaries of California are the richest farming region in the world, the largest manufacturer of commercial aircraft in the world, the birthplace of the Information Age—Silicon Valley—and the home of movie making and fantasy factories—Hollywood. Each are billion-dollar industries. Statistics from California's Office of Economic Research rank the state of California seventh among all the countries of the world in economic output. For two hundred years, stunningly, California's workforce has continued to make unprecedented leaps of paramount importance and has made history that has forever changed the future of this planet.

THE SILICON VALLEY

silicon / n. Chem. non-metallic element occurring widely in silica and silicates.

– Oxford English Dictionary, s.v. "silicon"

Stanford students William Hewlett and David Packard met in the 1930s when Frederick Terman, Stanford's famous professor of electrical engineering, arranged for them to meet. The two students borrowed $538, set up shop in a garage in Palo Alto, and through innovative technology and management that encouraged individual creativity, they built their company, Hewlett-Packard, into one of the most innovative and admired companies in the world. During World War II, the company produced radio, sonar, radar, nautical, and aviation devices. In 1969, Hewlett inspired the first pocket calculator, which entered the company into the strange and new world of computers.

In 1970, Paul Jobs made a telephone call to Hewlett-Packard on behalf of his son, Steve, in hopes of finding him a summer job. Steve Jobs was a child so charming and charismatic that he often held people spellbound. In another part of the same town, Steve Wozniak was a child so engrossed in mathematics that his mother sometimes had to physically shake him out of his mathematical musings.

After graduating from Cupertino High School, Steve Jobs traveled to India to do some soul searching, lived on a communal farm in Oregon, and enrolled in and dropped out of Reed College. He returned to California and ended up back in the Santa Clara Valley, where he went to work as a video programmer for a company called Atari and made some new friends at the Homebrew Computer Club.

Growing up, Steve Wozniak had two possible goals: he wanted either to become an engineer or a fifth-grade school teacher. He went with engineering and majored in it at Berkeley but dropped out in the mid '70s and began working for Hewlett-Packard. At that time, he became involved with a group of Palo Alto computer zealots who called themselves the Homebrew Computer Club, and the two Steves met.

Wozniak, known as the Wizard of Woz, had already invented the "blue box," a pocket-sized telephone attachment that enabled free and illegal long-distance calling. Steve Jobs handled its marketing. Pretty soon, with Woz's focus on engineering and Jobs's on marketing, they set up an office in Jobs's Palo Alto garage and began working on a computer they named the Apple I. Jobs received an order for twenty-five. To raise the capital needed to make the machines, they sold their prized possessions: Jobs sold his Volkswagen van, and Woz sold his Hewlett-Packard scientific calculator.

Shortly after, they were president and vice president of their start-up company, Apple Computers. Their logo was a red apple with a "byte" out of it. That first computer sold for $666. Next came the Apple II with the Woz's improvements. Jobs got busy promoting. Talk about pioneers. They launched an industry that has changed the history of the world and touched nearly every life in it—all from a place in California that has come to be known as Silicon Valley.

THE DRIVE TO SUCCESS

I am a California native, of African-American descent, raised in San Carlos, a part of the Bay Area.

My father is an electrical engineer, and when I was in about the seventh grade, we put together a little kit-computer. It was kind of a junky little thing, but it was my first look at a piece of electrical equipment from the ground up. Through that experience, at that young age, I started to realize how I related to technology.

At about that same time, we had gone out to eat one night with a friend of the family. Somehow I became split from my parents and what came of it was, that on the way home, I ended up in the car with the family friend. The man driving the car had been the vice president of IBM, and he asked me what I wanted to be. I told him right then, I wanted to get an electrical engineering in computer science degree, my master's in business administration, and own my own company by the time I was thirty.

I am thirty now. I had my degree and my own company by the time I turned twenty-nine.

When I run into people who are around twenty-four or twenty-five, they find it shocking that I knew what I wanted from the time I was in the seventh grade. But I think that is the drive behind Silicon Valley. You will find very young people starting our own companies and creating things from our own ideas. In high school, we were already building our own computers. Silicon Valley is turning out a lot of millionaires in their mid-twenties. We are extremely driven and it starts young.

MARLIN SCOTT, San Mateo

HOLLYWOOD

HOLLYWOOD BEGAN IN NEW YORK at the turn of the twentieth century where, on the rooftops of Manhattan, Brooklyn, and the Bronx, a new form of entertainment was taking place. Thomas Edison had invented a camera that enabled still pictures to become moving pictures called "movies"! Talkies came later.

In 1903, the first moving picture, *The Great Train Robbery,* was shot in New Jersey. The nickelodeon cost a nickel and plenty of people paid it, making *The Great Train Robbery* a hit. Movies became big business. During those pioneering years, there were only a few picture companies of major importance, and they threatened to put any newcomers in the quickly growing industry out of business. So the newcomers to the movies moved to a faraway place known as "the West." Why West? For the consistent climate; the sunshine, which made outdoor and location shooting ideal; but more importantly, to be close to the Mexican border, where they hoped to quickly and inexpensively handle any lawsuits that might arise.

The new industry liked the looks of a small rural community at the outskirts of Los Angeles called Hollywood. But upon their arrival and after announcing their intentions, moviemakers found they were not welcome and faced signs that read "No dogs and no actors."

In 1914, a director named Cecil B. DeMille arrived in Hollywood to shoot Hollywood's first big picture, *The Squaw Man.* Soon other companies and directors followed. Florence Lawrence became the first moving picture celebrity, William S. Hart the first celebrity of "westerns," and Francis X. Bushman, a former sculptor's model, became the first matinee idol.

Another director, D. W. Griffith, was a pioneer in this new and growing movie business. He invented visual techniques such as the long shot, the close-up, and the fade-out. He also discovered America's sweetheart, Mary Pickford. Every movie that has ever been made since that time includes the contributions of D. W. Griffith.

The beautiful women and handsome men of the movies entertained, and slapstick comedians made audiences laugh. The glamour and illusion, the factory-made fantasy of Hollywood and the movies, created celebrities so powerful that they became Hollywood's royalty, known as the "stars." Soon their salaries matched their limitless allure.

Then Bell Telephone took an innovative step; they wanted to add sound to movies. After being turned down elsewhere, Bell approached the Warner brothers who were running a fledgling studio. The brothers liked the idea and agreed to take a chance on adding sound. The first movie to include sound and music was *Don Juan*, made in 1926, but it did not include the sound of its star's voice, that of John Barrymore.

The era of silent movies ended when the first "talkie," *The Jazz Singer*, featuring Al Jolson, was released. The movies had literally found their voice, launching an industry that would eventually touch nearly every person on the planet. Now that's entertainment! And the rest, as they say, is history.

AEROSPACE

TOUTED AS THE "Eighth Wonder of the World," the *Aviator*—Frederick Marriott's thirty-seven-foot, steam-powered, "lesser-than-air" vehicle—flew over San Francisco Bay for five minutes. The year was 1869 and many credit that as the first flight in the Western Hemisphere.

In 1918, a boy named Jack Irwin was fascinated by the flight of birds. Later in life, he eagerly studied the glider planes that were being built by students at Berkeley. He founded the Irwin Aircraft Company, where he and his workers assembled the 240-pound, 15-foot-long Meteorplane, the "World's First Light Sport Plane."

This air-flying phenomenon fascinated the entire world, and a lot of people across the planet dreamed of defying gravity and conquering the skies. California, again, was in the forefront.

The aerospace industry had its beginnings before World War I. The consistent climate in California was responsible for its development, along with plenty of available local labor and the interest in experimental business by local investors.

Glenn Martin and Allan Lockheed were the pioneers of California's aerospace business. Donald Douglas was an associate in Martin's company, and John Northrup was employed at Lockheed. Eventually these companies merged.

After the companies had established themselves, Douglas built two planes for the army; they made the first round-the-world flight in 1924. In 1927, another manufacturer out of San Diego, T. Claude Ryan, built the *Spirit of St. Louis,* in which Charles Lindbergh made his solo flight from New York to Paris. To compete with Ryan and other aircraft companies, Douglas and Lockheed developed planes with all-metal frames, retractable landing gear, and controlled-pitch propellers. Among others, these California firms developed new, successful models of aircraft such as the Douglas cargo planes, DC-2, DC-47, DC-54, and later the DC-3, a major passenger plane. Lockheed manufactured the P-38 fighter, a twin-engined all-metal transport plane they called the Electra. Consolidated Vultee developed "flying boats" for military and commercial passengers.

The Depression, which started in 1929, started to lift nine years later. In 1938, military orders from the United States and Europe began pouring in all over California in anticipation of the impending war. New plants were built in Downey, Long Beach, Fairfield, El Segundo, Santa Monica, San Diego, Inglewood, and other California communities. The workforce increased by 223,000 people between 1939 and 1943. By the mid-1960s, the aerospace industry employed over 400,000 people in California and by 1982, approximately 641,000.

Douglas remains the world's largest manufacturer of commercial aircraft. One quarter of the nation's aerospace production is in California with more than half of the aerospace employment in Southern California.

ROGER. OVER AND OUT.

I was born and raised in California, and with the exception of the war years, I've spent the majority of my seventy-seven years right here. When I was twenty, I worked at Vultee Aircraft. The year was 1940.

We built the BT-13, out of Downey, just before World War II started. I remember a plane called the B-24. It was a four-engine bomber built and tested at Consolidated in San Diego.

When Pearl Harbor was bombed, I knew what I wanted to do. I got into the Air Corps Reserve Program. Next thing you know, I was on a troop train en route to the Santa Ana Army Air Base. The train tracks went through miles of orange groves. Most of the troops didn't even know what kind of trees they were. "How would we know what they are, we're from Joysey," they said.

Pretty soon, I was a bomber pilot, flying overseas in Italy, with my own crew, in my own California-made B-24 aircraft. We called it "The Liberator," and I named mine the "Nita Nell," after my girlfriend back in California. I spent a lot of time in B-24s—flying in them and bailing out of them. The guys in our squadron and I said, "Roger. Over and out" so often that I joked if I made it home alive, I would name my first son Roger.

I made it back home to California just before the war ended and moved to Vacaville. I flew a Sky Master, the C-54, made by Douglas. They were civilian-type planes that had been converted into hospital ships. I flew nurses, medical supplies, and medicine

overseas to the South Pacific and brought back wounded troops to San Francisco. We wanted to get our boys good hospital attention back at home, here in the United States.

I remember my last mission.

All airmen had to wear oxygen masks, and we all hated them. They were tight, and if you didn't have a close shave, it felt like cactus rubbing on your face for six hours. On the day of my last mission, I could see our base out in front of me, maybe five miles away. I opened my window, took off my oxygen mask, and threw it out, right into the propeller.

All that work we did in the state's aerospace business really paid off. We built good planes. But it sure felt good to come home to California and get my feet back on the ground, where I married Nita Nell, named my first child Roger, and ended up raising my family of five right next door to the orange groves I'd passed years earlier, on the way to serve my country.

JOHN OAKLEY, JR., Santa Ana

That Inventive Spirit

California is a state with a worldwide reputation for progress. People come from all over to educate themselves in technology and engineering at California Institute of Technology, UC Berkeley, and Stanford University. As more and more inventions receive worldwide recognition, the valley once known as Santa Clara is becoming known throughout the world today as Silicon Valley, a place where a lot of entrepreneurs are busy changing the world.

William Hewlett of Hewlett-Packard invented the audio oscillator, which provided an accurate source for low-frequency signals that is essential to the work of inventors, researchers, and scientists. Hewlett's first order was from the Walt Disney Studios, which used the oscillator in producing the soundtrack for the film *Fantasia.* Today Hewlett-Packard is one of the most admired companies in America. The State of California declared their original Palo Alto address "the birthplace of Silicon Valley."

★   ★   ★

Where was the first public school in the U.S. to receive consistent instruction by a computer? Brentwood Elementary, 1966, in Palo Alto.

The birth of something called the Internet was sparked in 1969 from the campus of UCLA as a way to communicate campus to campus. Leaders of the pack were Leonard Kleinrock, a professor of computer science, and a group of pioneers who called themselves the Advanced Research Projects Agency.

Kary Mullis. Sound familiar? Think back to the infamous O. J. Simpson trial. Mullis invented PCR, the process for amplifying nucleic acids that allows scientists to identify a fragment of genetic code, DNA, from a single drop of blood or from a hair. Mullis's patent was sold to the Swiss company Hoffman-LaRoche for $300 million, making it the most money ever paid for a patent. Kary Mullis is a surfer and lives in La Jolla.

From 1928 until his death in 1957, Ernest Lawrence worked at the University of California, Berkeley. By conducting himself with confidence and entrepreneurship, Lawrence climbed from associate professor to professor of physics and director of the radiation laboratory in two years. Lawrence invented the cyclotron. In case you don't know what that is, just know that without it most of the advancements in nuclear physics for the last fifty years would not have happened. For it, Lawrence won the Nobel Prize in 1939. In 1958, after briefings in Washington and on the way to Geneva, he was rushed to a hospital back at Stanford where he died. In his memory, the Ernest Orlando Lawrence Award is awarded to people for their inventions and other outstanding works.

California inventions that are somewhat less scientific:
the Barbie doll
blue jeans
the boysenberry

The microprocessor, one of the most important developments in the last half of the twentieth century, was invented in the same place a lot of other great stuff was invented— Palo Alto. In 1971, two men, Stanley Mazor and Federico Faggin, developed a single microchip that had as much computing power within it as that of a room-sized computer. Virtually every computer, automobile, and medical device in the modern world uses a microprocessor.

Native of Iran, scientist from Berkeley, Nina Bissel was one of seven people awarded the E. O. Lawrence Award from the U.S. Department of Energy for her work in breast cancer research. She is a cell biologist and became Director of Life Sciences Research at the Lawrence Berkeley National Laboratory in 1992.

Some of our tastier inventions:
   natural soda
   white zinfandel wine

Robert Bower of Santa Monica earned his degrees at UC Berkeley and the California Institute of Technology in Pasadena. While working at Hughes Research Laboratories in Malibu, he developed the Field-Effect Device with Insulated Gate, known equally confusingly as the Self-Aligned Gate MOSFET. Don't be discouraged. You don't have to understand it to benefit from it. This invention is the primary device used in nearly all integrated circuit designs. It is the device that provides semiconductors with the speed they need to serve in microelectronics. Bower was a 1997 inductee into the National Inventors Hall of Fame. Bower holds twenty-four patents and is currently a professor at UC Davis.

Add to the list:
  the pill
  the computer "mouse"
  the vaginal sponge

Here's some California problem-solving you can benefit from at home. When Irish coffee was first introduced to America in a San Francisco tavern, the cream wouldn't float. So dairy owner and mayor, George Christopher, along with his associates, found a solution to the problem. They let the cream stand for forty-eight hours and then frothed it, kind of like pancake batter. It still works, if you make sure your glasses are stemmed and preheated. Enjoy!

Lee De Forest was an inventor with three hundred patents. He worked for the Federal Telegraph Company in Palo Alto, where he developed intercontinental long-distance telephoning. Can you just imagine prices THEN? De Forest died in Hollywood after spending three more decades inventing stuff like color TV.

TV trivia: Palm Springs has the highest percentage of cable TV subscribers of anywhere in the country.

The first practical videotape recorder was invented by San Francisco-born, San Jose State graduate, Charles Ginsburg. It revolutionized television broadcasting.

Born in Los Angeles, graduate of Stanford, Theodore Maiman invented—the laser! In so doing he revolutionized medicine.

More remarkable inventions:
  the wetsuit
  theme parks
  the national bank credit card

Out of all the nation's biotechnology companies, sixteen percent are found in the San Francisco Bay Area, eight percent in San Diego, and five percent in the Los Angeles–Orange County area. Altogether 1,442 biotechnology companies call California home.

FIRST, RICHEST, OLDEST (ETC.)

Built in 1854, the Weaverville Drugstore in Trinity County is the oldest continuously operated pharmacy in the West.

Mr. Fuller opened his first of many Fuller Brush Paint stores in Sacramento.

San Diego, Los Angeles, and **San Francisco** are three of the top ten cities in the nation with the highest percentage of female business owners.

Sally Ride was a talented athlete who dreamed of a professional tennis career, but according to her mother, she couldn't aim the ball with consistency. So instead she became the first woman in space. In 1973, Ride graduated from Stanford University with a degree in physics. She applied to NASA, which was looking for scientists and technicians to monitor the very complicated technology for the seventh ride of the space shuttle, the Challenger. Eight thousand people responded to the announcement, one thousand were women, and Ride was one of the six women chosen. "The thing that I'll remember most about the flight is that it was fun. In fact, I'm sure it was the most fun I'll ever have in my life," Ride said later.

What was the first ice cream on a stick? It was the Eskimo Pie, which was invented for the 1932 Los Angeles Olympics. It sold for a dime.

If you measure success by wealth, then John Walton of the Wal-Mart fortune is at the top of the list in California. The number two wealthiest Californian is Lawrence Ellison, president of Oracle Corporation.

1975. Coalinga. The year and place that Kay Good became California's first female police chief by taking over their six-man force.

Blue Diamond in Sacramento is the world's biggest almond processing plant. On a busy day during a harvest season, over twelve-million pounds are delivered for processing from around the world.

Zasu Pitts and James Gleason were the actors in the first televised, full-length feature film. *The Crooked Tree* aired over a Los Angeles station in 1933.

Julia Morgan, born in San Francisco, was a woman of many firsts. After graduating from Oakland High, she studied at the University of California, Berkeley, where she became the first woman to graduate with a degree in civil engineering. She went on to Paris to again conquer and claim. Morgan applied to L'Ecole des Beaux Arts, where no woman had ever been accepted, and became the first woman to be granted a certificate. She returned to San Francisco, opened her own office, and became the first woman in California to receive an architect's license. Morgan designed many notable buildings in the state and was one of the most prolific architects in the Bay Area. She designed over seven hundred buildings, including Hearst Castle in San Simeon.

The first Shakey's Pizza Parlor was built by Sherwood "Shakey" Johnson when he converted a grocery store into a pizza place in Sacramento. Legend according to Shakey's is that it was the first pizza parlor.

Ma Bell it wasn't. The first telephone directory to appear in the West was in San Francisco. It consisted of 173 names and no telephone numbers. In those days, one asked the operator for the party with whom one wished to be connected.

The Golden State's largest retail mall is the Great Mall of the Bay Area in Milpitas, Santa Clara County, and is equivalent to the size of fifty-two football fields. Wear your sneakers.

Weinstock's department store in Sacramento was established in 1874 by David Lubin. The store first opened in a ten-by-ten-foot room over a basement saloon.

The nation's largest revenue-producing mall is Fashion Valley Shopping Center in San Diego.

At Beale Air Force Base near Marysville, the SR-T1 flies at more than three times the speed of sound. I didn't hear that.

Berkeley was the first city in America to mail education pamphlets on AIDS to every household in the city. The mailing was in 1987.

The first California-related stamp was issued in 1913.

The busiest library in the nation is the Los Angeles Public Library.

The first fortune cookie—1916.

The first public hospital in California was in Monterey and operated with two nurses and a burial squad.

WHERE HEALING HAPPENS

LOMA LINDA UNIVERSITY MEDICAL CENTER is an impressive, massive institution that could boast of many firsts, bests, and greatests. The $85-million Proton Treatment Center and the International Heart Institute, where the first infant heart transplant took place, are only two of Loma Linda's long list of internationally recognized medical departments.

Pushing the limits and daring to care is a philosophy and way of life born of the heart. The people of Loma Linda could, if they chose, boast about all of the lives that they save, but they don't. Rather, they take the position that it is spiritual power working *through* them and their hands that allows miracles to happen.

This is the story of how the devastating events of two people's lives caused them to cross paths and how, through their service to God, they developed a medical philosophy and way of life that resulted in six hundred medical institutions that reach seventy-three countries. The story begins over 150 years ago in the 1830s, a time when our approach to medicine was in desperate need of a change. At that time, the sick were relieved of their fevers by being bled with leeches and bloodsucking worms. It was during that time that two pioneering spirits, one regarded as a hero and the other as a prophet, lived.

John Preston Kellogg, his wife, Mary, and their four children lived on the prairie in Michigan, where they were poor and in ill health. Because of the grossly underdeveloped field of medicine and a prairie doctor's advice, John Kellogg was prescribed a wasp sting to the back of his neck to remove inflammation from his eyes. Mary had tuberculosis. She told her husband that if she should die, she wanted him to ask Ann, their neighbor, to take her place raising the children. After being bled periodically, Mary did die after giving birth to their fifth child. Unable to care for a farm, a home, and five growing children alone, Kellogg asked Ann to marry him. In two years time, they had a baby of their own, who also died because of the prairie doctor's negligence. John and Ann Kellogg believed their new baby had a lung infection, but the doctor insisted that it was worms. After a "purging," their baby died in convulsions. Ann insisted on an autopsy, which showed lung inflammation and no worms.

Ellen Harmon White was African American and suffered because of it. One day when she was walking home from school, nine-year-old Ellen was hit in the face by a rock and fell to the ground unconscious. She had been threatened, chased, and then dragged home, where she lay semiconscious for three weeks. She could not breathe through her nose for two years. Worst of all, for Ellen, was the event's traumatizing effect and the realization that her appearance made a difference in the treatment she received in the world. She could no longer retain what she studied in school. Her nervous system was so shocked and her struggles so difficult that her teachers advised her to leave school.

Ellen White grew up into a spiritually enlightened and remarkable woman of high consciousness. She lived her life in the service of God and made so many predictions that came true that, after many years and many truths, her church, the Seventh-day Adventists, considered her a prophet. One of her visions was that the Seventh-day Adventist church should have its own medical institution in which to teach and practice its philosophy of healthful and spiritual living. She and the congregation went to work raising the funds that the institution would require.

By this time John Kellogg had sixteen children and was making seventy-five cents a day working in a broom factory. He was a also a member of the Seventh-day Adventist Church. John Kellogg's life had been forever scarred by American medicine, so when he was asked by the appointed fund-raiser what he was willing to contribute for a new medical institution, he answered with determination, "five hundred dollars." The fund-raiser was thrilled and ran over to the White residence, where

Ellen White also pledged five hundred dollars.

Loma Linda University Medical Center in San Bernardino County is a result of Ellen White's vision and John Kellogg's determination. In 1903, Ellen White wrote, "True education means more than the pursual of a certain course of study. It means more than a preparation for the life that now is. It has to do with the whole being, and with the whole period of existence possible to man. It is the harmonious development of the physical, the mental, and the spiritual powers. It prepares the student for the joy of service in this world. . . ." She also wrote, "Godliness—godlikeness—is the goal to be reached." And concerning those who would work at the medical institution, she wrote, "The conduct of the workers, from the head manager to the worker occupying the humblest position, is to tell on the side of truth. . . . Our devotion to God's service is to impress those who come to our medical institutions."

Loma Linda University Medical Center is a hospital that includes institutes of cancer, transplantation, heart, orthopaedics and rehabilitation, the Childrens Hospital, and a level 1 trauma center. The hospital has over nine hundred beds. In addition, advanced degrees are offered by the Loma Linda Schools of Medicine, Religion, Nursing, and Dentistry. Also offered are curriculums in emergency medical care, physical and occupational therapy, radiation technology, radiation therapy technology, medical radiography, medical technology, respiratory therapy, speech-language pathology and audiology, cardiovascular perfusion technology, cardiovascular technology, medical sonography, and nuclear medicine technology.

Loma Linda has now graduated more physicians who have become medical missionaries than any other school of medicine in the world.

A MATTER OF LIFE AND DEATH

One of the last things I remember is being lifted up into a helicopter. Just before I lost consciousness, I heard the paramedic say, "We're taking her to Loma Linda," and then I vanished into a void.

From behind my eyelids, I was becoming conscious. I felt tightly bound, like a mummy. I thought that I was dying, and then I heard my mother's voice. Inside my head, for the first time, I spoke to a God I did not altogether believe in. I heard my mother demanding assurance that I would live through the night. I thought, "I should not be hearing this." And then I heard my father gently hush her. He said, "This is the best trauma center in California," but I did not know where I was.

For the first time, I heard one doctor's voice, taking command. He said, "My name is Dr. Bunnell. I will be your daughter's surgeon." And this man began to run down a list of injuries that surely were not related to me. While he was telling them that among other broken bones my spine was injured and I may not walk again, and that my lungs were punctured and I may stop breathing, I was more impressed with the sound of his voice than what he was saying. I could not see him, but I knew that I liked him. It is very difficult to explain how the flash of one moment can change the rest of your life. But that was my moment, inspired by the voice of one man, whom I could not see.

I survived injuries so catastrophic that my chances of surviving were 50/50. I will be eternally grateful to the kind, compassionate, and loving caretakers at Loma Linda. I remember at one point feeling somehow ashamed because so many people really seemed to care about someone they didn't know at all. I survived five surgeries, two years of physical therapy, an emotional breakdown, spiritual confusion, and then a new enlightenment that came from very nearly dying. Not only was my life saved, it was forever changed. Nothing as I saw it before has ever again been the same.

Not too long ago I walked, proudly, into Dr. Bunnell's office. He smiled, I hugged him, and he called me his "miracle patient." And then he said something strange. He said, "How is your relationship with God these days?"

Without hesitation I answered him, "Every day I thank you and God for my life. In that order."

He looked embarrassed and looked down. He held out his hands and while we both looked at them, he said, "These are my humble hands. Any good I do, I do because God works through them."

ANONYMOUS

Big Business Numbers

Big is not always better. However, California is a big state in a big country. Its population is big, and a large number of businesses are bringing in big numbers.

★   ★   ★

"Chi happens." There are over four thousand licensed acupuncturists in the state.

The Annual Red Bluff Bull and Gelding Sale in Tehema County is the largest of its kind in the entire nation. Over 1,600 animals are judged and sold to over five thousand cattlemen.

The first meeting to discuss the possibility of starting the transcontinental railroad took place in 1860 above a hardware store in downtown Sacramento.

If the San Francisco Bay Area stood alone, it would have the fifteenth largest economy in the world.

In 1993, fund-raisers collected $193 million from charitable people. In under nine years, over $10 billion were spent on lottery tickets.

Safeway, Lockheed, Disney, Northrup-Grumman, and Bank of America (recently acquired by NationsBank) are five of California's top twenty employers.

Two of the world's ten largest computer service firms are in California: Computer Sciences in El Segundo and Hewlett-Packard in Palo Alto.

There are approximately 103,000 active physicians and surgeons in the Golden State.

There are a lot of parents out there saying, "My daughter, the lawyer." There are more female partners and associates in L.A. and San Francisco than the national average. In 1930, there were more than 10,500 licensed attorneys in the state, and by 1995, there were another 107,000. Out of the ten largest California law firms, five are based in Los Angeles and five are based in San Francisco.

Of the top five hundred Hispanic businesses in the United States, 23 percent are in California.

It would seem there is a need for advice. Abigail Van Buren, who lives in California, receives ten thousand letters a week. Her column, "Dear Abby," appears worldwide, reaching 90 million readers in 1,200 newspapers.

The place to camp is in California. In one year, 8.6 million campers contributed $1.9 billion to the economy and provided 26,500 jobs.

The wine country of the north produces a lot of work. In 1997, 144,000 tons of grapes were crushed in Napa County alone.

Wanna buy a car? In 1994, there were 6,076 used car dealers.

California's state and local employees are the second highest paid in the nation.

There are 5,896 female pilots in California.

Workers paint year-round on the Golden Gate Bridge. It is so big that by the time they finish one end, it's time to repaint the other.

Located east of Barstow is the largest solar power plant in the world.

You can read a book while waiting for your diamond to be set in any one of the state's 1,722 bookstores and 3,119 jewelry stores.

MY BEST FRIEND WINI

Recently I was looking through an old picture album and came upon a picture of two little, six-year-old girls standing knee-deep in a field of California poppies. Their arms were full of the bright golden flowers.

One little girl had curls, full cheeks, a happy smile, and generated energy. The other little girl was thin, wan and pale, with a shy smile. Her left leg was in a cast all the way down to her foot and could be seen through the flowers. The girls were best friends and were happy to be together in the warm sunshine and in a sea of blazing, shimmering, shining California poppies.

I was the little girl with the endless energy. Wini was my best friend. She had polio and was forever crippled because of it. I loved Wini, and I loved the responsibility of taking care of her and seeing that she was always included and never left behind.

As I looked at that photograph and remembered that day, I wondered if in those early days my future was written.

Thirty years later, I worked for a large, national, nonprofit organization: a health agency providing funding and services to persons with disabilities, from babies to senior citizens. For twenty-four years, I served the organization. I became one of the first women executive directors of that time and was recognized as being in the top 5 percent of professional women in the United States financially.

Did Wini and those blazing California poppies help blaze the way to my future? I think so.

RUTH CAUDLE, Santa Ana

OLD MEETS NEW

THE PARADOX OF CALIFORNIA can be experienced by taking a drive across the state and witnessing the different industries present in the different areas. During such a journey, one can travel back and forth between two hundred years of California's history. Tooling along, with a glance out the window, can take you through hot fields with a Mexican flavor, to sleepy, salty beach towns, into ultra high-rise and bustling cities, right back to yesteryear and Cannery Row. Keep moving north through forests of redwoods and cities that once thrived on the timber business, and you will find you have traveled full circle, where California's past and future meet. The house that Juana Briones built in 1847 was one of the first homes built in California. It is still there today and it stands off Arastradero Road in the birthplace of the Information Age, Palo Alto.

The lumber business was booming at about the time gold mining pooped out in Del Norte County. For an entire century, an ample supply of redwoods (also known as the tall trees) sustained Crescent City as a timber port, but today most of the mills are silent.

As early as 1870, assorted timber companies began purchasing land around what is known today as Humboldt Lagoon State Park in Humboldt County, but the area remained unlogged until the 1950s when Louisiana-Pacific Corporation built a mill just east of Big Lagoon. In 1969 then-president Richard Nixon and then-governor Ronald Raegan stood next to conservationist Lady Bird Johnson when she gave the dedication speech for the newly formed Redwood National Park.

Canning is another big business that has become high-tech in California. Of the many packing houses and canneries of Northern California, the story of what happened to Santa Cruz Fruit and Olive Canning serves as an example of canning progress in all of California. It was founded in 1914 and operated until 1933. It was then purchased by a larger company, Pacific Coast Producers, a cooperative that was originally designed as a frozen food facility with a small canning line. Years later, they were canning green beans and pears. The one-time canner that had once hand-moved every single can became a "plant" with mechanized technology capable of producing 1.3 million cases of pears and green beans a year. In 1989, because of the land's value, the Bronson Street cannery ran its last can of pears. It was purchased by a group of investors and is now a business park.

Sun-dried grapes make Sun-Maid raisins, an old-fashioned California product that carries sunshine and health in a package to the world. How many pounds of grapes make one pound of raisins? Four and a half. Kingsburg is located in the central part of the Central Valley, which is the largest raisin-producing region in the world. In August, when grapes are at their sweetest, farmworkers painstakingly hand-pick bunches of grapes then carefully lay them next to the vines on trays made of paper, where they dry in the sun for two to three weeks. Growing and harvesting raisins is one of the most labor-intensive businesses in agriculture. Sun-Maid employees keep busy processing and packing millions of pounds of raisins in packets ranging in size from 1/2-ounce to an 1,100-pound container. Raisin packages are printed in fourteen different languages.

Juana Briones was born in 1803, during a time when California was still a remote outpost of Spain. She was a pioneer settler of Yerba Buena, which was later named San Francisco. Juana Briones raised cows, sold produce and milk to crews of ships, and ran a tavern. But she was most well-known for her skill and compassion when tending to the sick and wounded. She turned her home into a haven for people in need and gained income from those who could afford her medical services. When she was forty-two years old, she bought 4,439 acres of land called Rancho La Purisima Conception for $300. The area is known today as Los Altos Hills.

Only three families have lived in the house that Juana Briones built over 150 years ago, and it stands in Palo Alto.

1931 DESERT COFFEE BREAK

Even for a happy ten-year-old, playing on the farm during the summer in Imperial Valley was a hot situation! Because of temperatures well over 100 degrees, steam seemed to rise right out of the fields of melons. The ground was so hot it made blisters on my feet.

I couldn't wait to run over to the big shade tree by the barn where the stone-made olla (pronounced Oi-ya), full of cool, clear, refreshing water sat on a high table. A metal dipper hung from its side. I had to stand up on a chair to submerge the dipper in the olla. I took big, long gulps, letting the water pour over my face and down my clothes. Nothing could have been better!

Every farm had an olla—for the workers in the fields. That cold, sparkling water served as their life-line in that desert heat and was the coffee break of the day.

ANN JOHNSON, Imperial Valley

A DREAM COME TRUE

A couple of years ago, I was in Seattle for my sister's gradua-
tion. After the ceremony, our family all went to a restaurant to
celebrate. During the course of the meal, someone posed a ques-
tion. He asked, If we could go back to college and study something
different, what would it be? I knew immediately. When it was my
turn to speak, I proudly announced, "Broadcasting." The response
that I received was amazing. One person said, "Why would any-
one want to do that? It is so difficult to get into that line of work.
The odds of making it are very slim. It would be better if you chose
something in the computer industry, which has many more avail-
able jobs." And everyone agreed!!! I couldn't believe my ears!
How could they be so negative? How could they sit there and
crush my dream? I vowed silently to myself never to let others
influence me and never to let others tell me what is best for me.
Only I know that. I knew I needed to follow my dreams. I would
prove them all wrong.

I came to California knowing that pursuing television broadcasting
was something I needed to do. California is the land of opportu-
nity where literally anything can happen. The only problem was, I
was getting older. Not too old, but I was no longer in my twenties.
Could I be successful at that age? I decided age was not a consider-
ation, and I needed to follow my dream at any cost. I was excited
at the idea of going back to school and doing something that I had
wanted to do since I was a kid. Fear had stopped me in the past,
but not this time. All systems were go!

They say when you put an idea out in the universe, the universe perks up its ears. That is very true. I told a friend of mine, whom I trusted, that I was going to be a reporter and soon after, things just seemed to fall into place. I got an internship at a television station and started to sit in on meetings and editing sessions. It all helped. Less than a year later, my instructor at school told me about a job opening for a reporter. I met with the news director and was hired on the spot. I have never looked back, and I have never been happier.

It really is true. If you follow your heart and work hard, anything is possible. Anything! I am living proof. Never let others discourage you from your dream, because when it comes down to it, our dreams are all we have. And dreams do come true!

JEANNE BERGH, Santa Maria

California Cuisine

To UNDERSTAND CALIFORNIA'S culinary history, one only needs to look at California's cultural history. California cuisine is, like the rich diversity of people who make up this state, layered with ethnic flavors. It is unique, fresh, and always changing.

Although California cuisine is a recent phenomenon to the rest of the country, its development has been a long time in the making. Californians have always eaten differently. Not only do we have an elaborate assortment of cross-cultural dishes to choose from, California agriculture is the most productive in the world. We grow fifty percent of America's fresh food! It's true, fruits and nuts abound. And vegetables too. California leads the nation in seventy-four crops.

The staple diet of the first Californians, the Indians, was made up of acorns, berries, corn, squash, beans, and pumpkins, all eaten with whatever wild game or fish could be caught. The first Europeans to arrive, the Spanish, brought with them, among other things, garlic, olives, chili peppers, artichokes, dates, and grapevine cuttings. Eventually the Indian and Spanish influences evolved together, making a distinctive and exotic style of cooking that included fresh cheeses, olive oils, fruit preserves, grilled fish and meats, and spicy stews.

The gold rush sparked the biggest mass migration in the history of the world. Within weeks, California was deluged with fortune seekers from Europe, China, and other parts of the world. The East Coast states sent their fortune seekers as well, and all of these people brought their recipes and longing for the foods of their homeland.

Ramshackle lodgings served grub to the immigrants who also brought along their original trades. Among them were winemakers, dairymen, cheesemakers, chocolatiers, fishermen, farmers, and bakers. San Francisco and Sacramento became boomtowns. The railways, developed in the late 1800s, connected East and West coasts making cargoes of vegetables and fruit, especially citrus, available to a much broader population.

Chefs who had, from the turn of the century, offered heavy, American country fare, began changing their menus and preparing haute Euro-style specialties, which blended an assortment of unique California produce and our more relaxed style.

The birth of Hollywood, and later the '60s movement, strongly affected the world, this country, and the development of our state's fare. It was in the early '70s when a woman named Alice Waters opened a restaurant called Chez Panisse in Berkeley that the marriage of California organic and ethnic gourmet really began to mature.

Today California is home to some of the finest chefs, restaurateurs, and restaurants in the country. People come from far and wide to experience this fine food.

But it is we who live here who reap the culinary benefits of the now internationally recognized and admired fusion called California cuisine.

Fruits and Nuts

How often have you gone to the market and not found what you wanted in the produce section? In California it is more common to find such a large selection that it becomes difficult to make a choice. This variety of available, abundant food is wonderful for preparing and celebrating healthy, delectable meals and dishes.

★　★　★

The U.S. artichoke capital is Castroville, north of Monterey. The artichoke, which is related to the thistle, was first brought to America by Italian immigrants who settled near Half Moon Bay. (Once upon a time, artichokes were worn around the neck and planted in churchyards to keep evil spirits away.) Artichokes flourish in the cool, coastal climate. They can be sliced, sautéed, stuffed, boiled, or braised. There are over three hundred different preparations for the artichoke. The simplest, it is agreed by many, is the best; boil the whole artichoke and then dip its petals in clarified butter.

A good thing goes a long way. The hamburger originated with Turkish tribes who shredded low-quality beef and added flavors to make it taste better. Sometime before the fourteenth century, the dish was introduced to Germany, where it was a variation of beef Tartar, spiced and served raw. Later, German immigrants brought it to America. Sure, we grow organic and are health conscious, but we also love our burgers!

The first "drive-thru" was built in Baldwin Park in 1948 by Harry Snyder, when he dreamed up a classic by mixing two of California's favorites, burgers and cars. He had the unique idea of a hamburger stand where customers could drive up and place their order through a two-way speaker box. The result? In-N-Out.

In the late 1800s, Julian was a mining town. Located inland from San Diego, Julian is now known for its autumn apple harvest. Orchards surround the town. When fall festivals celebrate the fruit, the aroma of baking apple pies and hot cider waft through the old mining town's crisp, mountain air.

There are 3,333 bakeries in California.

There are several claims to the origin of Caesar salad, and one of them is California's. After his discharge from World War I, Alex Cardini from Italy joined his brother, Caesar, in Tijuana, Mexico. Caesar was the proprietor of a restaurant in which Alex created a salad to honor the pilots at nearby Rockwell Field in San Diego. In the beginning, it was called "Aviator's Salad," but later the popular dish took on the more personal name of Caesar's salad.

Date update: Dates originated in Morocco. Because of a date disease in 1920, Morocco sent over eleven palms to California in 1920. Today Indio is the largest date shipper in America.

The Pismo clam. You can still find them and take them home but only in appetizer size. The clams were once so plentiful that 45,000 a day could be harvested. It takes over twelve pounds of still-in-the-shell critters to make one pound of clam meat. Today at Pismo Beach, you can take home ten clams—if you are licensed.

Speaking of shellfish, oysters come to mind. The only true West Coast native is the Olympia oyster. Tomales Bay is home to three excellent oysters, the Belon, the Hog Island Sweetwater, and the Olympia. The Belon, prized and popular in France, and the Olympia, also grow in the waters of Eureka.

Edible fungi, the mushroom. It is celebrated and considered a luxury. Shitake mushrooms are grown in San Diego and are a treat that can be incorporated in sauces, salads, stews, and gratins.

The most honey produced in the nation is, that's right, here in California. South Dakota, the first runner-up, produces half as much.

Onions. Can you imagine cooking without them? The Golden State produces the largest crop in the country. They are basic to all broths, stocks, and soups. My favorite side dish, creamed pearl onions prepared with a dash of nutmeg. TIP: A slice of cold onion placed on a bee sting helps to stop pain and swelling.

Walnuts were first introduced to California in the 1700s by the Spanish padres. Long, long before that, they were traded as a delicacy from ancient Persia to Italy, Spain, India, China, and Japan. In 1860, the walnut industry was launched in California. Today all of America's commercially grown walnuts are from California.

In 1997, enough strawberries were grown in California to circle the earth fifteen times. One of the reasons we produce 75 percent of the nation's strawberries is our climate. In some regions, they can be harvested year-round. The great chef Careme created the dessert Strawberries Romanoff while working for Czar Alexander of Russia. The original recipe called for ripe strawberries crushed in a crystal bowl. A good red Port was poured over them, and after being cooled overnight, the mixture was forced through a sieve and then poured over fresh strawberries—into a larger crystal bowl, I would imagine.

There's abundance and then there's abundance. About 27 percent of the world's pistachios and half of earth's raisin supply come from California!

Cherry: a sweet, heart-shaped berry with moderately firm flesh. Hot cherry pie, crumbly crust browned to perfection, vanilla ice cream melting in the bowl. Pardon me, I got sidetracked. California is one of the top three cherry producers in the nation.

California produces 90 percent of the nation's apricots.

More nut numbers: almonds are the number one food export from California.

All these fabulous crops. This must be the reason California is referred to as "the land of fruits and nuts." All of these things and much, much more are available and waiting at the 21,300 restaurants in California.

STYLE AND TASTE

Alice Waters graduated from UC Berkeley in 1967 with a degree in French cultural studies. She trained in London at the Montessori School and traveled the following year in France, where the French approach to dining made a dazzling impression on her.

Back home in the Bay Area, Waters and a group of friends decided to open a neighborhood bistro with the goal of doing things the way a proper dinner party at home would be done. They opened Chez Panisse in Berkeley in 1971. The restaurant is named for a character in a trilogy of French films by Marcel Pagnol.

Right from the beginning, Waters has been concerned with, and has remained loyal to, environmental issues, believing that the best tasting foods are ecologically sound and organically grown. She contracts with over sixty nearby suppliers who are also concerned with environmental harmony.

It was nearly thirty years ago that Chez Panisse opened. During those early days organically grown and ecologically sound concepts were a radical departure from traditional thinking. Conservative menus were the norm of the day. Waters's innovative approach and enthusiasm made her a leader in the development of the now internationally recognized and admired "California cuisine."

In 1986, Alice Waters was named one of the ten best chefs in the world by the magazine *Cuisine et Vins du France*. In 1992, she was awarded "Best Chef in America" and "Best Restaurant in America" by the James Beard Foundation.

The Louvre chose Alice Waters to open a restaurant at the Paris museum. They are currently involved in negotiations.

Austrian-born **Wolfgang Puck** was first inspired to cook by his mother, who was a hotel chef. He began his formal culinary training at fourteen and apprenticed at L'Ousteau de Baumaniere in Provence, France. Shortly after that, he worked at the Hotel de Paris in Monaco and Maxim's in Paris where he further developed his distinctive culinary creativity.

In 1973, Wolfgang Puck came to the United States. Soon after that he became the star chef and part owner of Ma Maison in Los Angeles. He opened Spago on Sunset in 1982.

One year later he opened Chinois in Santa Monica, where the menu is a fusion of Californian and Asian. Granita in Malibu and Postrio in San Francisco feature elaborate Mediterranean-Californian menus.

Puck is one of the premiere influential chef-restaurateurs responsible for developing new trends in California cuisine. His gourmet line of frozen pizzas and his Pizza Cafes can be found in a variety of locations, including major markets and department stores all across the country.

Thomas Keller was born in Southern California but first gained recognition in New York, at La Reserve and Restaurant Raphael, where he earned national exposure. He is a veteran of several of the finest restaurant kitchens of the world. He served an *estagière* apprenticeship throughout France in the kitchens of Michael Pasquet, Guy Savoy, Gerard Besson, Taillevant, and Le Toit de Passy.

Keller, at forty-three, opened French Laundry in the heart of the Napa Valley in 1994. He received the Restaurants and Institutions 1996 "Ivy

Award," in addition to the James Beard Foundation's "Best Chef: California" award in 1996. In 1997, Keller was named the "Faberware Outstanding Chef of the Year," the highest honor given to an American chef by the James Beard Foundation, making him the first chef to ever receive consecutive "Best Chef" awards in the foundation's history.

French Laundry is considered one of the best, if not the best, restaurant in America.

CHEZ PANISSE

Chez Panisse is a house on a commercial street in Berkeley. You could drive right by and miss it, because the front of it is latticed with a big Thomason pine. A couple steps off the sidewalk, where the front yard might once have been, is a little brick patio with some benches, an outdoor waiting area.

A few more steps up, through the front door, and you enter the downstairs Chez Panisse, which seats thirty or forty, has two chefs, and its own kitchen. Downstairs has a prix-fixe meal. I think they know maybe a week in advance what they are planning to serve each night. It's a different menu every night. It might cost $45–70 per person. Reservations are often made two, three months in advance. Up until recently there were no reservations taken until 4:30 P.M.

Chez Panisse continues upstairs—a stairway that is so narrow that if you want to become friendly with someone, you can do so simply by walking up the stairs when someone else is coming down them. Now you are in Chez Panisse Café, which has same-day

reservations only. Downstairs only dinner is served. Upstairs both lunch and dinner are offered. When you first walk in, there is a bar and a seating area in the middle of the room. Behind the bar is an open kitchen, so you can stand and watch the cooking. Salads, entrées, pizza oven—it's more casual upstairs. The tables are covered with white butcher paper on top of white tablecloths.

Every day the chefs go down to the Oakland Airport, which is about twenty minutes from Chez Panisse, to receive crates and bushels of fresh vegetables from one or two farmers that have been growing organically for them for years. The standing order from Chez Panisse is, "Send us every day whatever looks the best." Whatever they take back with them was picked yesterday. They stand there on the tarmac, knowing what seafood and fowl they have received, and they design the evening menu based on whatever is in front of them.

Chicken and veal are favorites. They've been ordering a certain amount of chicken from the same guy, for, forever. Fourth generation free-range chicken. Free-range chickens of the American Revolution. Anyway, they don't serve chickens from dysfunctional families.

They cook the evening meal in the afternoon, and then Alice Waters will go through and taste it. If it's not to her liking, changes will be made. There have been times when something is deleted from the menu because it's just not up to snuff. She's tough like that. And mostly that's a good thing. People that work there will tell you that.

If I have a choice between rent and dinner at Chez Panisse, I go to Chez Panisse. No, but I go once a week, sometimes twice, and before I leave I always draw a cartoon on the butcher paper. It's a caricature of the kind of person, the kind of waiter, the kind of customer; it's about the attitude, not the person.

I always put a circle of either tea from the bottom of my tea cup or wine from my wine glass, and write either "The Zinfandel Stain of Authenticity" or the "Earl Grey Stain of Authenticity." Usually they take my cartoons and they roll them up and put them up in the back—the staff takes turns keeping them.

One day, after a late lunch, I was sitting there while they were setting up for dinner. This time I drew something different because it was their twenty-fifth anniversary. I did a big rococo, fancy, swirly, giggly, CHEZ PANISSE and then a big "25 YEARS of no reservations till 4:30." They cleared the table, rolled up the cartoon, and as I was getting ready to leave, all of a sudden this little lady comes by—short hair, little pillbox hat, big roll of butcher paper in her hand—and says, "Thanks for my drawing!" I looked up and it was Alice. I said, "Thank you for years of great food! I didn't know you'd seen my drawing." It had never occurred to me that Alice had ever seen any of my drawings, but she said, "I never miss them. I insist. It's one of the rules!"

McNair Wilson, San Francisco

Say Cheese

Over two hundred years ago Father Junípero Serra, the Spanish missionary who established twenty-one California missions, became the founder of our agriculture industry by introducing many varieties of vegetables and fruits. He also brought with him the art of cheesemaking.

When gold was discovered in the next century and the rest of the world discovered California, many who came were from cheese-producing countries. Today California is the nation's leading dairy state.

According to legend, when a shepherd boy went on his daily rounds and left his milk pouch in the sun, way, way back in 4,000 B.C., the heat and enzymes coagulated the milk. The pouch was made from sheep stomach, which contains rennet, and behold, cheese was born!

★   ★   ★

Danish pioneers established Ferndale's dairy industry in 1852. Today the town is still known for producing butter. When Portuguese and Danish dairymen built houses they became known as "butterfat palaces."

Clarissa Steele from New England made the first commercially successful cheese in 1857. She missed the taste of the cheddar cheese she had enjoyed at home, and so, with recipes from her grandmother's cookbook and by obtaining milk from wild cattle, she began making cheese. Within a year, she and her family were selling Steele Brothers Cheddar in San Francisco.

Laura Chenel began making goat cheese with her herd of twenty goats in Sebastopol. A wine and cheese shop in San Francisco told her she must go and see the owner of Chez Panisse, Alice Waters, and show off her cheeses. After everyone had tasted them, Waters ordered sixty a week. Today Chenel has 350 goats that produce nearly a half million pounds of cheese a year.

A baby Holstein calf weighs about one hundred pounds and can walk within one hour after birth. A cow must be a mother first before she will produce milk.

From the island of St. George in the Azores came Joe and Mary Matos. They settled in Sonoma County, where, from the herd of cows that live between their driveway and their factory, they make a full-flavored, semihard cheese called St. George Cheese.

Basque sheepherders once operated a cheesemaking farm near Mt. Tamalpais in Marin County.

Nancy Gaffney received a goat from a friend in 1976, which, eight years later, had turned into a herd. Soon she was making goat cheese along with fifty products called Sea Stars Goat Cheese. They include a beautiful, edible flower petal-covered chevre. What was once a "trendy" California cheese is now available nearly every-where across the country.

There are 800,000 cows working for you, producing milk, in California.

Monterey Jack cheese was pioneered by Spanish settlers who called it "queso blanco."

David Jacks, as in Monterey Jack, was the first to market this cheese in 1882. Monterey Jack is the most famous of the California cheeses.

A milking Holstein cow weighs between 1,100 and 1,500 pounds and produces 19,825 pounds of milk a year. That's 2,305 gallons a year and eight gallons a day during her milking period—enough for 128 people to have one glass a day!

Hispanic cheeses like Queso and Fesco are the fastest growing in the cheese industry. Other varieties of cheese include those that originated in Holland, France, Greece, Germany, Sweden, and Portugal.

The black and white spots on a Holstein are like fingerprints, no two have the same pattern.

HOT DOGS AND KALBI

Nearly born but wholly raised in Los Angeles, I'm the mix of everything that this town holds. L.A. is probably home to almost every ethnicity in the world. And in this hodgepodge mixture of people, I found my little niche.

Hot dogs and kalbi—the perfect mix. Kalbi are Korean-style ribs, marinated in a mixture of soy sauce, sugar, pepper, and garlic. Birthdays were great 'cause there was food and presents galore, and these occasions gave my dad a reason to barbecue like there was no tomorrow. The smell of burgers, hot dogs, and kalbi made my chubby kid body eager to be the first in line. It's funny to reminisce about the days of yore, when all I needed to be happy was some good food and a little attention. As I grew up to experience all the sociology and ethnic-American studies courses a college campus had to offer, I can say that those days growing up in my funkily colored peach and blue house perfectly describe who I am today—that blend of Korean and American.

I remember that when I turned nine, my parents threw this neighborhood shindig and invited a family that was unfortunate to have a red-headed, freckled punk for an eleven-year-old son. He sampled one of the kalbi strips and pretended to gag, making fun of the unfamiliar taste. Right then, I felt so ashamed that my parents cooked such "ethnic" food. And I also wanted to make that boy the recipient of my newly learned karate moves, the little weenie.

Isn't it great what hindsight allows you to see? So, yeah, I've thought about that boy from time to time, and I've imagined countless scenarios in which I inflict some kind of embarrassment or pain upon him. But my point is that that little skirmish set the stage for creating a consciousness about my place in this world. Pretty heavy thoughts for a nine year old, but I fancy myself precocious back then.

Anyway, these parties are the events that I hold accountable for creating my outlook on being a first generation Korean American. I grew up in a city fortunate enough to have diversity, which taught me to appreciate my parents' contribution from their native culture. And now, I experience a new kind of culture, sprung from my home culture of Korea and my host culture of America. But I must say, I think L.A. has got a culture of its own.

MINDY CHUNG, Panorama City

Mexican Specialties

Restaurants come and go. They open and close as owners, prices, and menus change. However, occasionally a good one will stay. One of my favorite restaurants is La Chiquita Mexican Restaurant (formerly known as Joe's), which has changed very little in twenty-five years.

During my entire childhood, every Friday night we had "Joe's." My mother phoned in the order and my dad went to pick up the food, which was on heavy paper plates, wrapped first in tin foil and then put in brown paper bags. I always ordered the same thing, a beef taco, sometimes two, and a bean tostada, please. Although the Friday night tradition stopped a long time ago, rarely do I make a trip home to visit my parents when we don't visit La Chiquita.

Joe, the original owner, sold a few years ago, and he sold to a group of loyal customers who have been eating at the restaurant as long as my family has. Part of the deal before the new owners signed across the dotted line was that the menu and the recipes would never change.

★   ★   ★

Huevos Rancheros. This dish extends back to the days in California when travelers were served eggs (and other things) from rancheros, also used as rest stops. Today huevos rancheros means a hearty breakfast made up of a combination of fried or poached eggs, refried or black beans, tortillas, cheese, and a spicy sauce.

Hungry? The biggest burrito ever made was at Rengstorff Park in Mountain View. It weighed 4,456.3 pounds and was 3,578.8 feet long. Why? Good question.

El Tepeyac is famous for Manuel's Special Burrito. This three to four pounder was developed for the Cal State Los Angeles football players who used to come in really, really hungry after their games. Nothing else on the menu filled the fellows up, so the owner started making foot-long burritos. If you could finish it, it was free. But the offer caught on and ordinary folk with football player appetites came in and gobbled away. The burrito is still made with rice, beans, green chilies, guacamole, and cheese, but today, whether you finish it or not, you pay. El Tepeyac has been in business for forty-three years.

Pretension works when bottling wine and chilies. Larry Watson, who settled in the wine country of Northern California, became interested in chili peppers. He was living in Cholula, between Vera Cruz and Mexico City, when his appreciation of chilies began to grow from watching his friend Justino make chipotles by smoking and roasting jalapeños. What started off as a way of making fun of winemakers' attention to detail by using descriptions like "I blend my chiles to fill the entire mouth," ended up a successful business of pepper sauces called Bustelo's. The label on each bottle reads, "The pungent capsicum-acetic acid solution is intended for gastric and aphrodisiac stimulation."

Here is a recipe that dates back to the Aztecs: vanilla and chocolate combined in drinks. Latin markets carry a good Mexican brand of chocolate called Ibarra.

Chips and salsa anyone? This combo is to California what mayo and white bread is to the Midwest. Pico de gallo, chunky salsa with extra cilantro, is a personal favorite. The delicious dip can be found at most salsa bars and hundreds of our Mexican food restaurants, seven of which are rated the best in America.

The margarita was invented in 1947 by bartender Al Hernandez and Morris Locke, who owned the La Plaza Restaurant in La Jolla. They came up with the combination mixing lime juice with Jose Cuervo Gold and French Cointreau. Salud!

TAMALES

I was born on June 4, 1954, in Stanton, California, a few blocks from Disneyland. Juan and Consuelo Machado, my parents, came here from Mazatlan Sinola, Mexico. When my parents moved to California, they brought with them many traditions. One of those traditions was making tamales.

Tamales are made in my family once a year on Christmas Eve. As far back as I can remember I woke up to the smell of the chile and carne (meat) cooking over the hot stove. I remember my mother kneading the masa (corn meal). I believe this is the hardest part of making tamales. You are over a big pot, and you are kneading the masa over and over. You have to get both your arms in the masa in order to knead it well, and so you are up to your elbows in it. It takes about an hour and a half to get it to the right texture. I remember my mother pouring the broth from the hot pot of carne and adding it to the masa. You could see the steam coming from the masa when the broth hit it. It smelled so good!

According to old Hispanic legend, the masa is the heart of the tamale. If you can master that then you will succeed at making the perfect tamale. Meanwhile, the hojas (cornhusks) were soaking in the sink. They had to soak for hours in order for them to be soft so that next we could fill them with the masa, carne, chile, and a vegetable.

We had a little assembly line going, and of course back then the men never helped. My mother said that it was a woman's job. I remember thinking how unfair that was. I mean, we were all going to eat them, so why can't my brothers help? The girls would gather around the kitchen table, and my mother and two older sisters would spread the masa on the hojas and pass it down to us. One of my sisters would put the carne in, then she would pass it down to my little sister and me. We would add the vegetable then pile the tamales at the end of the tables until all the tamales were filled. Then we would tie each tamale separately.

My mother would assemble them in a BIG cooking pot, and that is when my father would get involved. It was his job to cook them outside and make sure that they did not burn. As a child, I didn't appreciate this hard work at Christmas time. I didn't realize that this was a tradition passed down to my parents from generation to generation. My mother stopped making tamales when my father died. You could say that the tradition of tamales died too.

Now as an adult and a mother of two girls myself, I have continued the tradition in my own home. I want my girls to know that some traditions should continue, even though we complain about the hard work involved. Once we taste the first batch of tamales, we all agree on one thing, we realize that it was worth the hard work and the wait.

I also added a new tradition of my own. No matter if you are a man, or a woman, or a child, if you want to eat tamales, you WILL help make them, or you will find something else to eat on Christmas day.

MARTHA VICTORINO, San Jose

The San Francisco Bread Story

DURING THE LATE 1800S, many new things from countries older than ours were introduced in California. In San Francisco and Oakland, that included three bakers of French bread named Parisian, Colombo, and Toscana.

This was during a time when people, in the process of coming from all over the world to settle here, were still learning about the promise of California. During that time of growth, bakeries were able to send their drivers out by horse and wagon to deliver bread to folks from door to door as a part of their service.

By the late 1930s, the automobile had long since replaced the horse and buggy, and bakeries were using trucks and vans to deliver their goods. Then by the 1950s, bakeries were delivering to grocery stores and restaurants.

Parisian, Colombo, and Toscana merged in the 1970s and became San Francisco Bread Company, which is today the largest baker of sourdough and French bread in the world. Over two million loaves are baked weekly. Do you know about the unique guarantee in the bread industry? The baker serves a store or restaurant with bread one day and then gives full wholesale credit the next day for anything that wasn't used or sold. This started as a way to encourage sales and entice new customers. The guarantee continues today.

This California product can easily be found throughout our state, but something very special remains about actually being in the city where it is made, knowing your fresh, warm loaf of bread was baked right where you are. A loaf of San Francisco sourdough bread is a slice of California history.

FOOD TIDBITS

Everything is bigger out West. In 1853, a guy in San Francisco stripped the feathers from a dead ostrich, cut off its head, separated and tied its legs, then labeled it "California Turkey."

Chinese soup in early nineteenth-century California was made with opium, but not enough to break the law.

How much did you last pay for abalone? The Chinese, ahead of their time (or maybe Californians were behind), loved it and ate it when it was inexpensive and frowned upon in the 1880s.

The Colusa Rice and Waterfowl Festival is held in November each year to celebrate ducks. The annual California State Duck Calling Championship is held in Colusa County. No quack jokes, please.

This is not something that European winemakers probably promote, but in the 1870s a blight nearly wiped out the vineyards across much of Europe. California roots and cuttings were exported and account for most European wines.

Two men in a fight over legs. Frog legs that is. In Calaveras County, in 1878, John Blackburn killed Frank Deschaux over an argument about the correct way to fry frog legs. Talk about temperamental chefs.

Parties aren't what they used to be—in Sunnyvale, anyway. In 1881, the Marty Murphys invited the state—the entire state, I say—to celebrate their fiftieth anniversary. Seven thousand people (give or take a couple hundred) showed up. They came from far and wide and must have been hungry. Eighteen barbecued cows, fourteen sheep, ten pigs, and a carload of roasted chickens were consumed and washed down with a freight car of champagne and six hundred gallons of other drinks. Oh. And they stuffed a bear and sat it at the head of a table, but at that point do you think anyone really noticed?

They called it loyal then, we might call it obsessive-compulsive today. Louis Lurie liked Jack's Restaurant in San Francisco so much that he ate lunch at the same table every day for thirty-four years.

Rumor, not legend, has it that while under the influence of something called alcohol, Fatty Arbuckle, at the Vernon Country Club, put a steak between two slices of bread and devoured it all. The steak sandwich and another pound was born.

I'm telling you, people just don't know how to have fun like they used to. In 1915, pilot Lincoln Beachley of San Francisco was known for flying upside down. A dinner party was thrown, upside down, in his honor. All the food was served upside down, and he was carried in upside down and tried to eat standing on his head. Prohibition was when?

SNOW IN SOUTHERN CALIFORNIA

It was Thanksgiving of 1994. My friends' family and my family decided to celebrate Thanksgiving in a different way.

Mt. Laguna, at an elevation of 6,000 feet, is one of the prominent mountains in the Quiamacha Mountain Range in San Diego. That is where my family and our friends decided to celebrate Thanksgiving.

We made reservations to stay at a campground at the top of the mountain. The reservations were not necessary. Nobody was there but us. There we began the most unusual, most memorable, and most exiting Southern California Thanksgiving.

After setting up camp, we began preparations for our feast. As the turkey was smoking and the potatoes were roasting, the air temperature began to drop. By the time all the food was ready, it was beginning to get dark. The seven of us sat quietly around the fire eating. The food was so good, none of us noticed that it was getting very cold out. After we were finished eating, we told stories long into the clear starry night.

Later that night, when we were sleeping comfortably in our tents, the temperature dropped below freezing. When we woke up, we were pleasantly surprised to see snow gradually falling to the ground like feathers. None of us had the remotest expectation to see snow falling in the county of San Diego. Southern California is a very unpredictable place. Snow on Thanksgiving is a perfect way to sum up the unpredictability and uniqueness of California.

JOE TENENBAUM, San Diego

The Gilroy Garlic

Rudy Melone, an Italian who came to Gilroy in the late 1970s, knew of a small town in France that attracted eighty thousand garlic lovers per year to their garlic fair. In addition, they claimed to be the garlic capital of the world. Well, Rudy knew a ridiculous claim when he heard one and went to Don Christopher of Christopher's Ranch. Together, in 1979, Don and Rudy started the Gilroy Garlic Festival. The head chef of the fest is Val Filici, who learned how to make sauces at six while his parents worked late at a cannery. Today the Christopher Ranch is the nation's largest fresh garlic grower, the Gilroy Garlic Festival is the most successful community festival in America, and Gilroy is the garlic capital of the world!

★　　★　　★

Garlic is native to Siberia.

The largest garlic ever grown was grown in Eureka in 1985 by R. Kirkpatrick. The gigantic bulb weighed in at two pounds, ten ounces.

Garlic was so highly valued in ancient Greece that fifteen pounds bought a good strong slave.

Alice Waters of Chez Panisse dazzled critics at a New York press luncheon featuring new young chefs by bringing little heads of lettuce still in their garden soil all the way from the West Coast of California. In addition, she roasted whole garlics, making herself, her preparation of garlic, and Chez Panisse famous.

Garlic is mentioned in the earliest Sanskrit writing.

Garlic is a member of the lily family.

Calorie count: one to two calories per clove, eight to ten cloves per bulb. That's a lot of inexpensive, low-calorie flavor!

THE SMELL OF WAFFLES

You know how sometimes you have a favorite song throughout the years, and at one point or another, you hear it and it reminds you of a good time in your life—a girl that you liked—maybe a bad time or a turning point in your life? For example, when I hear "That's the Way of the World" by Earth, Wind & Fire, I think of high school and, in particular, a girl that I went out with my senior year. Well, that's how I feel about food—in particular, waffles and bacon and eggs. Especially when I hear my aunt's voice sing out from downstairs, "Boys, breakfast is ready!"

My Aunt Sue (my mother's sister) cooks the best buttermilk waffles in the business. To this day, whenever we have a gathering of family or friends, and my aunt asks me what I want for breakfast, I am the first to shout out, "Waffles!" (Like she had to ask.) And just to savor the moment, I stay at her house overnight so that I can wake up in the morning and not only smell the aroma that permeates my senses but hear her voice over the intercom telling us to come and get it.

Food has dominated my family for a very long time. Just like in the movie Soul Food, *there's always something dramatic going on when there is a holiday, or maybe when a family member comes to town and we are just plain having a good time.*

On my mom's side of the family, there has been a rich midwestern tradition of family gatherings and the celebration of food. And when I was very small, my Uncle Cat and Aunt Della, who lived in Palmdale, would always have their big Thanksgiving gatherings at their house. Chickens, rabbits, and dogs would run rampant around the house, but that smell of turkey mixed with collard

*greens, mashed potatoes and gravy, and sweet potato pie leaves a
fond memory of feeling safe, having a good time with my cousins,
and listening to the old war stories Uncle Cat told. To this day,
whenever I smell holiday cooking, I think of those days in Palmdale, when life was good, I was protected, and nobody could ever
hurt me.*

*As the years went on, my Aunt Sue picked up where my Aunt
Della and Uncle Cat left off. From the time I was in junior high
right to this very day, some of the most special moments in my life
have been family gatherings. Breakfasts my Aunt Sue made for us
when we were growing up—that safe feeling. Uncle Merril, too,
telling his war stories and the smell of those waffles in the morning
as I lay wrapped up in bed waiting to hear Aunt Sue cry out,
"Boys, breakfast is ready!"*

BRIAN STEVENSON, San Bruno

The Classics

Los Angeles is a trendy kind of place where what's hot today is not tomorrow—where a classic restaurant is as cherished as a classic film. From the golden days of Hollywood were the Brown Derby, famous for its cobb salad; Cyrano's for its onion soup; and Romanoff's, famed for its chocolate soufflé. These legendary restaurants, like the era in which they thrived, have seen their final act. Of the great old restaurants only Chasen's and Musso and Frank's are left.

But a taste of yesteryear can still be experienced at a different sort of place. Built in 1908, when sandwiches were ten cents and the cent sign was a key on the typewriter, Philippe's Delicatessen still stands. Famous for their French dip sandwiches, Philippe's serves old-fashioned fare at fair prices on sawdust floors.

Philippe's started ninety years ago when Philippe Mathieu, a Frenchman from Aix-en-Provence, sold rolls, sliced meat, and condiments to his customers, who then put their own sandwiches together. One day Philippe accidentally dropped a roll into a pan of roasting juices, and, according to legend and the yellowed newspaper clippings hanging on the walls, the customer liked it so well that he asked his sandwich to be "dipped" again the next day. Behold, the French dip!

Today, for about $4.00 each, Philippe's sells fourteen thousand French dips a week. Other favorites are coleslaw, potato and macaroni salads, coconut custard and baked apple pies, and homemade doughnuts. Other items from the menu you may or may not want to miss are pickled pigs feet, pickled eggs, and corned beef and hash. For $10.00, a sandwich, salad, and a slab of pie will leave you with barely enough room for coffee, which is ten cents, but enough for a tip and a warm, fuzzy memory of yesteryear.

SUNDAY DINNERS AT THE LYNCHS'

*"Bless us, O, Lord . . . and pass the biscuits!"—a familiar
beginning to the weekly Sunday dinner at Una Lynch's house.*

*A mother of eight who immigrated from County Cork, Ireland in
1949, Una began her Sunday dinner tradition as a means of
keeping her family together. More inconspicuously it was a way
of keeping track of whom any one of her six sons and two daughters were "going around with." I began dating Una's fifth son,
Desmond, in the heyday of Sunday dinners—an experience for
those who have a taste for comfort food and a quick wit to match.*

*The evening would usually begin with one of the older boys seated
at the head of the table, setting the tone for whatever hazing of
newly invited guests would follow. Dinner always consisted of
well-done roast beef, peas and carrots, mashed potatoes and gravy,
and plenty of Una's legendary hot biscuits. A traditional Irish feast
if there was one! No one was ever turned away, and somehow
there was always enough food.*

*Dinner conversation was maintained at a dull roar, and expletives
were saved for when Una was in the kitchen preparing the next
course. After dinner, the dining room would quiet as teacups were
passed while several pots of tea brewed. At this point of the dinner,
Una would finally take a seat, with her hot cup of tea in hand.
The evening would end with the assurance of another delicious
Irish meal, lively conversation, and a hot cup of tea waiting until
next Sunday.*

ELLEN LYNCH, Calabasas

Julia Child

JULIA CHILD was born Julia McWilliams in Pasadena on August 15, 1912. At that time, across the country, Pasadena represented paradise, a perfect place where palatial homes and hotels housed members of the Valley Hunt Club. Those who could afford transcontinental travel spent the high season in style—in Pasadena.

Horsedrawn wagons delivered groceries, and the ice man delivered the way to keep them cold. Julia was a debutante who graduated from Smith College in 1934. During World War II, when her friends were getting married and raising families, Julia, an independent California spirit, volunteered with the Office of Strategic Services in China and India.

After the war she met her future husband, Paul Child, in Paris. It was because of Paul that her appreciation of French cuisine began. At thirty-seven, she began her culinary career at the Cordon Bleu. Soon after, she and two friends opened L'Ecole des Trois Gourmandes in Paris. After ten years of training and experimenting, she wrote *Mastering the Art of French Cooking,* her first of nine books. It was a bestseller and today remains the most authoritative cookbook for home chefs interested in French cooking. The book inspired the PBS television series *The French Chef,* which won an Emmy and a Peabody award. *The French Chef* was followed by several other series. In her *Master Chef* programs, Child is host to twenty-six of America's finest chefs and in *Baking at Julia's,* she is host to twenty-six of the country's finest bakers.

Some tips from Julia's kitchen are:

★ Learn the basics so that cooking is not a chore.

★ Always have a timer, sharp knives, and practical, good pots and pans.

★ Keep the pantry stocked with onions and potatoes. Keep the refrigerator stocked with eggs, butter, and olive oil. And a bag of mixed, grated cheeses to sprinkle. And milk and crème fraîche (which she makes herself). And bread. Oh. And be sure to put the bread in the freezer after you've baked it and it has cooled completely.

★ And lastly, eat together and keep the television turned off during meals.

Her favorite ingredient? Butter, of course.

Julia Child is now eighty-five years old and lives in Santa Barbara, California, and Cambridge, Massachusetts. She is a California woman ahead of her time. Both she and her career are legendary.

OLIVE OIL

IT'S BIG AND GETTING BIGGER, but it's not new. The first olives in California were called Mission olives. The trees were planted two hundred years ago by Franciscan padres at their mission in San Diego. Olives provided both oil for cooking and table fruit at the new settlements. Groves were planted all around the state from the Mission cuttings. Saplings came from Italy and France as well. The most common olive trees were Mission, Manzanilla, and Sevillano, all good for table olives but not the best for oil. Farmers found table olives more lucrative; they brought in double what oil olives did. Many of the groves of trees growing good olives for oil were abandoned or ripped up. As the demand for better tasting oil has grown and the health benefits of olive oil have become more recognized, the oil market has expanded steadily.

Ventura County produced the first commercial olive oil from Camulos Mills in 1871.

In 1900, the World's Fair was held in Paris, and California brought home the gold medal for olive oil.

How many table olives can a canner get for $750? About a ton.

Ridgely Evers was the first person in this century to import Italian-variety olives. His trees are from cuttings from the Luccese village of Segromigno-in-Monte. The olives and are called Leccino and Pendolino. They are handpicked and the oil is made in Mill Valley. Olive oil should be bottled in dark glass to protect it from sunlight and heat, which can alter the flavor. Olive oil should be purchased in amounts that can be used within six months or less.

Olive oils, whether refined, virgin, extra-virgin, cooked, or not cooked, all have health benefits. Save your less expensive olive oil for cooking. If your oil becomes so hot that it smokes, consider it rancid. Here are some ways to use your flavored or more expensive olive oil: drizzle over foccacia bread, use to pop popcorn, use as a dressing for an artichoke, toss with grilled red peppers, drizzle over tomatoes, mozzarella, and fresh basil.

Olive and canola oil are best for cooking because they are composed chiefly of oleic acid, a monounsaturated fat that is more resistant to the damaging effects of heat and light than polyunsaturated oils are.

At the northern end of Marin County, near San Antonio Creek, is the largest planting of Italian varietal olive trees in the state.

LUNCH WITH ELIZABETH AND NANCY

It's been a few years ago, about five, but it's something I'm not likely to forget. An ex of mine used to loan his jet to Elizabeth Taylor, and so they were friendly. One summer she rented a house in Malibu that was perched on top of a high cliff overlooking the Pacific Ocean. As the ex and I drove along Pacific Coast Highway looking for the address, I remember thinking that I heard music in the air. We located the house and as we drove through the gate, turning onto the property, a calypso band was playing on the roof of the main house. It looked just like the set of a stage. We giggled as we parked the car. At that moment, a golf cart arrived and the driver handed us each a beautiful turquoise and cobalt blue glass of cold Sangria. We were driven along the side of the house, down a long, narrow road that zigzagged steeply and directly down to the guesthouse on the sand.

The first person I saw was Elizabeth Taylor, our hostess, who was lifting a tortilla chip with a dollop of guacamole up to her mouth. I remember thinking this was a passionate woman who undoubtedly loved good food. Her hair was very black, her chin perfectly pronounced, her smile sweet and familiar. The party was very colorful and casual; we all removed our shoes in order to walk in the sand. It felt odd meeting Elizabeth Taylor in bare feet.

I remember all the food was beautifully prepared by Elizabeth's chef. There were Greek, Caesar, and tostada salads. Small, ripe olives and feta cheese, with cold, fresh cucumber in the Greek. I recall a very slight taste of anchovy in the Caesar. I wanted to just bury myself in the tostada, piled high with three different kinds of cheese, but I was wearing white. Chips and salsa with mounds of fresh guacamole were everywhere. Hot dogs, hamburgers, chicken—all grilled. There were plastic pails filled with flowers on the tables; the tables were all in the sand.

Nancy Reagan was sitting at a table alone. We were introduced to her and she was, well distant, I would say. And very thin. I kept watching to see if she would enjoy any of the wonderful feast, but I never saw her eat a bite.

It was such a beautiful day. It was a shame we had to leave. We went just down the road and had a late lunch at Geoffrey's, where I swore I could hear the sound of Calypso music floating down the beach.

Lou O'Toole, Pacific Palisades

♪ ♪ ♪

BARBECUES AND BASEBALL FOODS

THE WORD BARBECUE dates back to 1697, when the Taino Indians from the American West Indies roasted whole animals on a wooden frame called a "barbacoa." This was a way to celebrate on festive occasions.

Barbecues are to California what baseball is to America. Parks and neighborhoods are filled with folks gathered around their grills, while summer breezes carry Frisbees and woodsmoke. Hot dogs spit and pop from firepits in the sand. Days are long, nights are strong, burgers char, and corn on the cob roasts, their aroma drifting inland and all along the coast.

In the early 1800s, in the Sacramento Valley, ranchers celebrated their spring roundup by gathering together with neighbors and friends. They prepared hot coals outdoors and seared steaks and beef roasts that were served with what was then traditional fare: beans, salsa, and garlic bread. In Rancho Cordova, the Santa Maria Barbecue carries on the authenticity of the old days with their big, on-site barbecues, and buckboard wagons.

Nothing beats the flavor of mesquite charcoal or hickory chips for barbecuing.

Tofu burgers sold at the ballpark? Yes, and sushi too. Edison Field, in Anaheim, home of the California Angels, now has a gourmet restaurant from which fans can be served in the stands. Add to that a crepe stand and a sushi bar.

Fish tacos and Mexican specialties are favorites at Jack Murphy Stadium in San Diego.

San Francisco's 3Com Park offers forty kinds of food.

The Oakland Coliseum juices fresh carrots.

Have no fear! All of the ballparks still offer peanuts and hot dogs, and I plan to continue to eat mine with relish.

AND THE WINNER IS . . .

Marilyn Monroe, also known as Norma Jean, was the 1947 Artichoke Queen in Castroville.

A Carrot Queen is crowned every year in Holtville, a town with a population of 5,575 that lies east of San Diego and north of the Mexican border. Holtville claimed itself as the carrot capital of the world in 1948, when one in every three carrots in the United States was grown there. Holtville's one-time Carrot Carnival is now a yearly Carrot Festival.

The National Orange Show crowns a Citrus Queen every year in San Bernardino.

There is a Garlic Queen at the Gilroy Garlic Festival. The 1998 winner, Christina Carrier, won the honor partially because of her imaginative rewording of "Hey, Good Looking" to "Hey, Mr. Garlic."

Team California: The Culinary Olympics have taken place every four years throughout the century. California did so well in the 1996 competition that for the 2000 event, to be held in Berlin, the U.S. will be represented by two teams—a national team and a California team. Team captain Brad Toles says that California is considered the Hollywood showoff team, even though in the 1996 event, California had the simplest display. Other countries spent $100,000 in lighting fixtures alone. California's display consisted only of the different regions within our state. We brought home the only gold medal awarded to the United States, including the official U.S. team, proving that when you've got enough of it you don't have to flaunt it.

FRENCH LAUNDRY

It's called French Laundry because, in fact, the building was at one time a French laundry. It was also a bordello at one time, but it is now one of the finest restaurants in America.

French Laundry is right off Route 29, which is the north/south route through the Napa area of the Wine Country. It's just north of the town of Napa in a little country town called Yountville. You couldn't it find if they described it to you. It's impossibly hard to find. When you get to it, you think you're not there. It looks like an old brown, brick, two-story, leaning to the right, Dickensian building with stuff growing out of it. There are louvered windows that are always closed so you can't see in. There's no sign, there's no number, but it is on the corner that they will tell you it is on. And you will get there and you'll think, "That can't be it." There's no parking lot—it sits right on the corner.

There's a big backyard that has these big troughs that are probably four feet high, eight to ten feet wide by twenty feet long. There are probably four or six of these where they grow a lot of their own herbs and vegetables. There's an outbuilding, which looks like a garage, that actually is a brand-new building. This is the kitchen, and across one entire wall is a huge picture window so you can look into it.

There's seating inside upstairs and seating outside. Outside there are about a half dozen tables for two or four. In the summer time, you can sit outside, look into the kitchen and also enjoy the herb garden. It's just gorgeous.

Inside, it's like a little home. There is a reception area—a bar that's very nonplus. So you've got this nonplus exterior, then you walk into this nonplus reception area and you say, "I still think we're in the wrong place." Because there isn't a bar with bottles stacked behind it—it's just a small bar with no one standing around it because that isn't necessary. They encourage you to arrive on time, and within a few minutes of arriving you are seated. It's very nice and very elegant, but it's sparse.

The candlelight inside makes comfortable lighting. They have a big staff. Everybody waits on every table, so there is a constant flow of things. There is always somebody standing nearby. None of the rooms are big enough that you would even have to signal. It's almost like the on-deck position. You can just look up, and someone will take care of whatever it is that you wanted. That impressed me as much as anything. I spilled some wine, and they came right over with a cloth that was larger than the napkin but smaller than the tablecloth. It was like getting a new tablecloth but more discreet than changing the entire cloth would have been.

Thomas Keller is the owner and chef. French Laundry offers three menu choices. The prix fixe, the semi-prix fixe, and what's called the "Chef's Tasting Menu." It's sixteen or eighteen items served one at a time—all of them gorgeously, flawlessly, colorfully prepared and arranged. They are a little bigger than bite-sized. But even before you get your first item off the tasting menu, six or eight other things come. Smoked salmon on toast points with a sprig of mint. And the tiny waffle cone, the size of your thumb, shaped like a rosebud vase, with a scoop of raspberry sherbet, bright red, and then a mint leaf—then a dollop of salmon roe. Things that do not appear in nature together. But you could taste everything. If there

were three or four different ingredients in an item, you could taste all of them. None of them dominated. Now keep in mind that with each course, every piece of silver is changed. About twenty-five different place settings passed before me by the end of my meal.

The wine by the glass arrangement is brilliant. You pay a $25 fee and they just keep bringing you wine. Sometimes you're finished with a course but half-way finished with the wine, and they say, "You're having the pinot noir now, sir. We've got a steak Tartar coming. Would you like a cabaret or zinfandel to go with that?" And you say, "Sure" and that glass goes away and a new, fresh glass comes. I probably had eight different kinds of wine during the course of the evening, probably the equivalent of four glasses. Dessert was probably six different items. I ended up having twenty-four or twenty-five things. I didn't even feel like asking about doggy bags UNTIL the bill came. Then I said, "I want the table, my chair, I want my napkin, I want that waitress." You know what though? The check arrives like a laundry tag, and when mine arrived, I never for a moment felt like it wasn't worth it. It's a lot of money for one meal, but WELL worth it."

CRAIG WILSON, Berkeley

TIME AND DOUGH ON MY HANDS

A few years back, twelve to be exact, I was between jobs with a bit of time on my hands. With a newborn son and a wife at the University of California in San Diego studying biochemistry, money was a bit tight. So there I was with a newborn, a two-year-old, and my wife. What should I do with my days?

It got to be Friday afternoon, and I got a bee in my bonnet to try something I had never done before. I tried to follow a recipe to prepare a challah (Jewish twisted eggbread). I figured that with two young sons and the future ahead, it might be nice to rekindle a Jewish tradition for our home of four. There was time to experiment, and we could eat the result!

The first go of it got me full of sticky dough—I had no idea that if the dough was too gooey I was supposed to add more flour! (The Jewish cookbook said nothing about this practice that every baker knows about!) While getting if off my fingers, I ended up washing half of the dough down the drain, but enough was salvaged to give us all a real taste delight.

As the years proceeded, I devised some superior methods for handling the dough (including having the boys taking turns pounding out the air and braiding the dough), and Friday evenings became a time that we all looked forward to with the aroma of the baking challah and the other intoxicating smells that accompanied it. We learned to celebrate the end of the week with the traditional sensations that have marked Jewish culture for hundreds of years.

HOWARD TENENBAUM, University City

How We Have Fun

No DOUBT ABOUT IT, we know how to have fun! With so many natural wonders to choose from, we seem to come by it naturally. With the beach out front, the mountains in back, and the desert in between, our Golden State has become a vacation destination for people all over the world. Add to the mix a generally fabulous climate, and the ingredients add up to fun—so much so that it is not uncommon to hear people from other states say, "You don't know how lucky you are."

Our ancestors came looking for work, seeking their pot of gold at the end of the western rainbow. And they brought with them their dreams. A large part of California's long-standing allure is that we symbolize the land of plenty where anything is possible and "the good life" can be found.

Although the pioneers brought with them a formality and moral sensitivity, the West has always had a reputation for being a bit wild, so it did not take long for a casual and relaxed lifestyle to begin to develop. Betting on horses and playing poker in saloons were popular pastimes, as were hunting, bull fights, and gun play out on the wild frontier. Ladies stayed at home and planned seasonal socials and parties, read poetry, and worked at fancy embroidery.

In those days, the poor and the leisured class partook in very different, and often separate, kinds of activities. But one thing that could be enjoyed by all were spectator sports. Since sports were considered to be character builders, everyone could root for the home team regardless of social rank. As a result sports became, and remain, a part of our public health.

Much has changed from those early days, but a lot remains the same. What has changed are the kinds of sports that are played, the numbers of people playing, and the gender of people participating in them. If you don't want to take part in sports, by surfing the waves or skiing the slopes, you can celebrate that which hasn't changed—the scenic range— just by taking a drive. Nature is a place to rejuvenate, a thing to celebrate, and we of the Golden State have plenty of opportunity for both.

Each year California presents hundreds of unique festivals that celebrate just about everything, from classic arts to frog jumping. Picnics, playgrounds, and parks are full year-round. Visiting all the different mansions and castles is another popular California past time. And if you're looking for something off the beaten track, check out our ghost and gold rush towns. The gold rush inspired Knotts Berry Farm, then came Disneyland, where millions of people come to visit yearly.

In addition, California is the fantasyland where hundreds of stars and celebrities choose to make their home. Star tracking is a favorite pastime too. Where else can you pull over on the side of the road to buy a map to the star's homes? But all it takes is a short road trip to find yourself out of the city and surrounded by desert, driving upon land that looks as though no visitor has ever tread upon it, or lost in the wilderness and giant redwood forests up north. We have so many choices of things to do that having fun has become an expectation. In California "nothing to do" is rarely an option.

California has so much to offer in so many fun-filled ways that it is a fantasy state where only our reality surpasses our folklore. Like our pioneering ancestors before us, we are the spirited and fortunate few who can start our own celebrations and create whatever we want to honor whatever lifestyle we choose. In so doing, we deepen our sense of awareness through community activity and deepen our love of nature by just being out in it.

Northern, Central, and Southern California all offer a plethora of fun-filled activities. What follows is a small sampling of what's to be done out there. If you've already seen and done it, then go ahead and think up something new. Chances are it will catch on. Everything starts somewhere, and very often it is right here in our beautiful backyard.

From the Mountains to the Sea

THERE ARE OVER FOUR HUNDRED BEACHES along our 1,200 miles of coast. There are so many fun activities to be enjoyed on our beaches that I'd run out of room trying to list them all. What's your pleasure? Swimming, body- and windsurfing, body- and surfboarding, catamaraning, yachting, diving, wading, looking for shells and whales, Frisbee throwing, girl and guy watching, or just laying in the sand soaking up some sun. How about some volleyball, a bike ride, a jog, a hike, or a walk? Afterward you'll surely be hungry, so bring your gear for fishing, a picnic, a barbecue, or how about a grunion hunt? Tired? For overnight fun, park your RV or pitch a tent and bunk down so you can wake up with the sun and do it all again.

The sixteen national parks we enjoy in California provide just as much fun as do our beaches. Yosemite, Sequoia and Kings Canyon, Whiskeytown-Shasta-Trinity, Lake Mead, to name just a few, offer a stupendous playground for outdoor fun. Like what? Downhill and cross-country snow skiing, water and jet skiing, snowboarding, houseboating, sailing,

kayaking, rafting, fishing, or just plain swimming. Hiking, biking, motor-
cycle riding, rock climbing, backpacking, or lots of watching birds, butterflies, bears, deer, or waterfalls. Wrap it up by drifting to sleep while
stargazing, snuggled up in your sleeping bag, eternally grateful to live in
such a state.

SUMMER OF FUN

*The most fun I ever had was the entire summer of 1974. My best
friend, Susie, and I were both from Orange County, both sixteen,
with blonde hair, hard bodies, a tan, and an attitude. We had so
much fun that our parents barely survived it.*

*The day after school let out, we took off riding in the back of
Susie's dad's camper which was pulling their fast boat. We flirted
and waved at every cute, young guy in a car that we saw, until we
had a line of cars following us to Lake Shasta and Susie's dad
wondering why. The fun never let up, and we stayed an entire
month. Susie taught me how to water ski and I taught her how to
dance. We had all the open space we needed, and when we weren't
fishing and flirting, we were skiing and dancing in the dark.*

*The following month we spent on the beach in Carlsbad. I taught
Susie how to bodysurf and she taught me how to drive stick shift,
which worked out well. All the surfers we met invited us to parties,
and I had to drive my dad's truck to get to them.*

*We drove up and down the busy coast, missing rare and cherished
parking spots from craning our heads to wave at guys whistling by.
The smell of the sea was everywhere. How we loved the taste of
salt on our lips and the sting of sunburn on our skin as the sound*

of laughter floated down the beach. Settling down on warm, grainy sand and looking down our long, brown legs, over our toes, to the light blue sky stretching across the ocean blue sea, we reveled in the beauty of those summer days.

We thought we owned wherever we were, and that summer, we were everywhere.

PAM VECTANACKS, Huntington Beach

THE HEAT IS ON

The score was tied one-to-one in the bottom of the ninth, with two men on, and I was pitching. I must not lose this game. I'd worked all summer to get into shape for this season on the pitcher's mound my dad built for me. We'd trained together for three months, he was catching and I was pitching, so that I could be in shape this season—and this season had boiled down to this one moment. If I could get just one more out, we could go to the tenth inning tied. As my dad and one of his partners sat in the stands watching, I remember looking at the full moon and thinking, ONE MORE OUT. *I had to either get the ball past the batter or place it in a position where he couldn't get the meat of the bat on it. I wound up, looked left to first base, right to third, and pitched a strike right between the batter's knees and the plate. I got the third out and pitched a scoreless tenth inning. The game was called because of curfew. Tied, one-to-one. The heat was off—until the next game.*

ROGER DILLARD, Temecula

Sports Stars

There are many different kinds of stars. There are, of course, celestial scatterings in the sky, and then the kind that showers California—movie, music, television, all of the arts, and sports too. We have a profusion, a plenitude of all. Here is but a wee sampling of our golden girls and guys, some homegrown heroes and sheroes, as well as local teams and tidbits, from one of our favorite pastimes—sports!

★   ★   ★

Lindsay Davenport, 22, of Newport Beach became the No. 1-ranked female tennis player in the world in 1999, the same year she won the ESPY award for best female tennis player.

Tiger Woods, who is from Cypress and attended Stanford University, had a good golf year in 1997. He set twenty records and tied six. And then he won the Masters Tournament.

Stanford champions, between 1912 and 1996, have won 159 Olympic medals, 90 of them gold.

Sinjin Smith, native of Santa Monica, won eight FIVB International Championships of Beach Volleyball, three World Championships, two Tournament of Champions, and two King of the Beach Invitationals.

What diver set a possibly unbeatable record by winning over one hundred major championships in diving? Greg Louganis from

El Cajon, graduate of UC Irvine. He also is a four-time Olympic Gold Medalist.

Jerry Rice of the San Francisco 49ers scored three touchdowns in two Super Bowls. After eleven seasons in the NFL, he had rewritten the record books. He held career marks for total receiving yards with 13,275, most pass receptions with 820, and most touchdowns with 139.

In 1995, a wild frog named San Francisco Warty-Niners won the Calaveras County Fair Jumping Frog Contest by jumping 18 feet, 3½ inches.

In baseball, Jose Canseco was the first Oakland A player to achieve back-to-back 100-RBI seasons.

Florence Griffith-Joyner, who attended CSU Northridge, won Olympic track and field gold medals in 1984 and 1988.

The world's first surfing museum is in Santa Cruz.

In 1980, Orange County's Mary Decker Stanley broke the four-minute mark track barrier for the 1,500-meter run.

Nolan Ryan, one-time Angel pitcher, threw seven no-hitters in his career.

John Elway, Stanford football star, was drafted by the New York Yankees as a second round choice. Two years later, he was picked in the NFL draft.

There are 305 public golf courses in California. Only Ohio and Michigan have more. The community of Palm Springs, population eighty thousand, has forty-two courses making it the reigning champion of the golf resort world, where over one hundred yearly tournaments are held. Pebble Beach Golf Course is California's most exclusive golf course, located at the south end of the Monterey Bay.

Micky Wright, from San Diego, she won more than fifty tournaments and ranks among the LPGA all-time greats.

Nancy Lopez, born in Torrance, won both the LPGA Rookie of the Year and Player of the Year in 1978.

Head coach Bill Walsh (1979–88) led "The Team of the '80s," the San Francisco 49ers, to three Super Bowl titles, (XVI, XIX, XXIII) in ten years. Walsh was famous for being an outstanding offensive coach and developed what is now known as the "West Coast Offense." He was born in Los Angeles and attended San Jose State University.

Paul Kriya of the Anaheim Mighty Ducks won the "High Standard of Playing" and "Sportsmanship" trophies both in 1996 and 1997.

Stanford had the most players drafted in the first (1936) NFL draft.

Jim Otto, Oakland Raider center, entered the NFL Hall of Fame in 1980 after many had labeled him "too small" to play football.

Corky Carroll of Surfside won over one hundred surfing titles, including three International Professional Championships.

Oscar De La Hoya of Los Angeles has won boxing championships in four different classes.

California native Peggy Fleming won the gold medal in women's figure skating. It was the only gold medal awarded to an American in the 1968 Winter Olympics.

Chad Hundeby, Irvine resident, broke the English Channel swim record in 1994 by swimming it in seven hours and seventeen minutes.

Horse trainer Bob Baffert of Huntington Beach won the Preakness and the Kentucky Derby in 1998 with the horse Real Quiet.

Kareem Abdul-Jabar has scored the most points of any player in the NBA—at 38,387. Wilt Chamberlain is second with 31,419.

Arthur Ashe, UCLA athlete, was the first African American to win Wimbledon and the U.S. Open. He was twice ranked No.1 in the world.

Long Beach native Billy Jean King became the first female athlete to earn more than $100,000 a year in 1971. She's come a long way baby, and her tenacity has allowed many female athletes to follow her lead and receive fair pay and play in the male-dominated sports world. She was awarded 1999's ESPN's Arthur Ashe Award for Courage.

Wilt Chamberlain, a one-time Laker, held forty-three NBA records. **Elgin Baylor, Magic Johnson,** and **Kareem Abdul-Jabbar,** also natives of California, all played for the legendary Laker basketball team.

Tennis star Tracy Austin, swimming superstars Johnny Weissmuller and Mark Spitz, jockey Willie Shoemaker, and baseball legend Joe DiMaggio are all California homegrown.

Four-sport star Jackie Robinson is the only athlete in the history of UCLA to win a letter in four sports. He was an all-time Dodger great, National Baseball of Fame inductee, and the first African American to play major league baseball.

Jackie Joyner-Kersee went to UCLA on a basketball scholarship and became the greatest female track and field athlete in the world. She won Olympic gold and silver medals and set five world records.

Disneyland

ARMED WITH HIS IMAGINATION and entrepreneurial skills, Walter Disney moved to California from the Midwest in 1922. One year later he and his brother, Roy, had established the Disney Brothers Studio. They later produced a cartoon feature called *Steamboat Willie,* their first commercial success which starred a character named Mickey Mouse.

The studio was soon producing other innovative cartoons and commercial triumphs, including the first feature-length animated film called *Snow White and the Seven Dwarfs.* In his career, Disney won thirty-two Oscars.

Early in the 1950s, Disney's roving imagination came to fruition when he purchased a 180-acre tract of orange groves in Anaheim. Disney and his staff of "imagineers" set about designing a "Magic Kingdom." Disneyland opened on July 17, 1955.

Visitors travel from every corner of the planet for the thrills and enchantment of Disneyland. If ever there was an example of the power of imagination and a dream come true in California, Disneyland is it. It is one more magical, California thing that adds to the rose-colored glow in the eyes of people all across the world when they wish upon a star to come to our state. "The happiest place on earth" to millions of visitors a year is in Anaheim, California.

★ ★ ★

OH BOY!

When I think about Disneyland the first thing I see is the big boulder on the Indiana Jones ride rolling into me. Boy, was I scared!

Over on Tom Sawyer's Island I remember shooting the guns in the fort, playing in the caves, and walking over the barrel bridge.

I really like the car ride because I get to steer. We go under roads, around turns, and I'm doing the driving! I am not alone—Mom or Dad are with me.

The jungle boat ride in Adventureland was scary because hippos came up close to our boat and the driver had to shoot them. Are they real?

When I was younger, I remember going through Mickey and Minnie and Goofy's house in Toontown. It rained that day, and we bought raincoats. I get real excited when I think of all the rides, and I'm very excited to go again. It makes me feel good.

CONNER KRAML, Age 8

Mavericks

THERE IS AN AREA OF BEACH in San Mateo County called Mavericks where winter storms create huge swells and waves up to thirty feet that can be lethal. Mavericks is considered one of the three best surfing locations in the world; the other two are Baja and Oahu.

Surfing originated in Hawaii, but all along the coast it is a very California thing. Anyone who knows it well, knows that it is more than just a sport. It is a religion where the ocean reigns supreme, where the perfect summer is an endless summer, and where every surfer dreams of riding the perfect wave.

SURFSPEAK

(In order as they appear in the following story):

going off: When waves are breaking consistently. **macker**: A really big wave. **gnarly**: Treacherous (same as **hairy** or **hairball**). **grommet**: Young or small surfer. **stoked**: Majorly excited (origin: as in stoking the fires of the heart and soul.) **swell**: A wave before it breaks. **west swell**: a swell traveling from west to east. **thick one**: Usually relates to how thick the lip of the wave is. **drop**: The downward slide after the takeoff. **sucked**: A wave that pulls back. **pitched**: When a wave throws forward. **threw**: Same as pitched. **reentry**: The surfer shoots to the top of the wave in a maneuver and then skates along the top just ahead of the curl.

THE RIDE OF A LIFETIME

Mavericks lies beyond the cliffs and a half mile out to sea from the north shore of Pillar Point. It is not the kind of spot anyone should surf alone. The lineup is one of the most spectacular sights there is both in beauty and intensity and that's before you factor in the size of the wave. When Mavericks is going off the waves completely crush the reef. They are mammoth, true makcers, they are gnarly, and can be lethal. Grommets be warned.

When we left the house that day to check it out I thought the season was over. As I watched from the top of the cliff I was stoked to see a new swell rolling in. The waves had a lot of west in them and were stark in their beauty. They rolled like thunder, major thick ones breaking in great long sections all over the place.

Dave and I paddled out and waited. Once out I began to wonder exactly who was hunting who. Me, a big-wave hunter or the killer waves, stalking me, the ocean's prey? And then I caught a macker. The drop was an intense rush. It sucked, pitched and threw. I eased a turn, water inches from my face. My re-entry was the best of my life. Over the top I pushed at fifteen-feet, water exploding at my heels. And then I pulled a long, full bottom turn.

It was the most awesome moment in my life of surfing. One wrong move and I would have been another Mavericks casualty. I can feel the adrenaline rush as I write these words. If you surf Mavericks you had better know and respect the forces of the ocean or it can kill you dead.

BO "EASY" DANES, Malibu

Festivals

What a festive and fun way to celebrate all of the wonderful things that make this the unique, quirky, abundant state that it is. California has a huge variety of festivals, each one providing us a way to applaud music, art, and theater, or show appreciation for hometown folklore from food to frog jumping. As usual, our weather, fertile soil, diverse environment, and cultures give us a multitude of choices, including festivals to attend.

★   ★   ★

Bach, Beethoven, or Mozart? Carmel celebrates the baroque music of Bach for three weeks, beginning in mid-July. Monterey holds two Mozart Festivals, one in July and the other in August. San Diego's Mozart Fest is in July. San Francisco presents a Beethoven Festival in June with performances by the San Francisco Symphony.

For less formal fun how about some frog jumping? Angels Camp inspired Mark Twain to write, "The Celebrated Jumping Frog of Calaveras County," which became his first published success. The Calveras County Fair, held in May, has a Jumping Frog Jubilee Festival, where three-legged contenders are favorites. Folklore contends these little fellas must be faster and stronger to survive in the wild.

Sacramento hosts the California State Fair and gets festive every August. Sacramento also hosts (annually over Memorial Day weekend) the Sacramento Jazz Jubilee. It started in the '70s as the Sacramento Dixieland Jubilee and soon grew to the largest Dixieland festival anywhere. It is a big event and lots of fun.

In the Shasta Cascade region, listen up for the Shasta Jazz Festival in April, the Siskiyou Blues Festival in July, and swing on by Tehama's Western Open Fiddle Championship in October.

In San Diego, the weather alone is worthy of celebration, providing lots of fun-filled San Diego days. San Diego's Street Scene, a street festival featuring musical acts from around the world, is held in the historic Gaslamp Quarter in September.

In Ventura, kick off your shoes and go on out to the California Beach Party in September, when longboard surfing competitions are held and long summer days are enjoyed. Surf celebration is not limited to surf towns. The Surf Music Festival is held at Mammoth Lakes in Mono County in August.

Many of the nation's flower seeds are grown in Lompoc, where they present the Lompoc Valley Flower Festival in June. The California Poppy Festival is held in April in Lancaster. April is also the month for Riverside's Orange Blossom Festival.

The debate continues as to whether Calabasas derived its name from the Indian words meaning "where the wild geese fly" or from the Spanish word for pumpkin, which is *calabaza*. Either way, the Pumpkin Festival is held in Calabasas in October. Did you know pumpkin is a fruit? It is, and so is the tomato—where in Fairfield, it happens to be a favorite. Fairfield hosts a Tomato Festival in August. If you have a really great asparagus recipe, you can enter it in Stockton's Asparagus Festival, which is held in April. On shady, lush lawns in Paso Robles, basil lovers can celebrate at the Basil Festival in August.

At the Winterfest in Chester, Plumas County, family fun is guaranteed at snow sculpture competitions, dogsledding, snowshoeing, and snowmobile racing.

In Turlock, the Viking heritage of Denmark, Finland, Sweden, Norway, and Iceland is celebrated. There is a traditional Italian Fest in Oakland, which includes a Saturday night dance under the stars. Modesto presents a Greek Festival, and in San Jose, the Ahi Matsuri Fest celebrates the coming of autumn at their Japanese festival. All are held outdoors and celebrate the different cultures by serving traditional foods, playing traditional music and having people dress in traditional costumes. They all can be enjoyed in September. Oakland's Chinatown Streetfest is held in August and is the largest Asian street fair in North America.

If you can't afford building a real castle, make one in the sand. The Newport Beach Sandcastle Contest draws participants of all levels.

Steinbeck and Shakespeare. The genius of Salinas-born John Steinbeck is honored at the annual Salinas Steinbeck Festival, held in August. Steinbeck won the Nobel and Pulitzer prizes. Salinas was the setting for many of his novels. The genius of Shakespeare's writing continues to be appreciated and honored at summer-long festivals in San Francisco, Santa Cruz, San Luis Obispo, and Carmel.

The Cherry Blossom Festival in San Francisco's Japantown is unsurpassed in pageantry.

The only sawdust you will see at the Sawdust Festival in Laguna Beach is on the ground. This unusual thirty-two-year-old festival presents artists and their fabulous handmade art from handmade booths in a village that is also handmade.

The Festival of the Arts and Pageant of the Masters, still going strong after sixty years, is another unique festival and pageant held in Laguna Beach, where people are painted to re-create masterpiece paintings. The grand finale is Da Vinci's Last Supper.

One out of every eight music festivals in the United States is held in California. Some of the best to mark on your calendar are:

April: Spring Opera Theater in San Francisco, four weeks of opera presented in English.

May: Sacramento Jazz Jubilee, three days of ragtime, Dixieland, and other jazz.

June: Playboy Jazz Festival, jazz greats perform at the Hollywood Bowl.

July: Music at the Vineyards in Saratoga, three weeks of little-known classical works.

August: Idyllwild Music Festival, two weeks of orchestral music.

September: Monterey Jazz Festival, the oldest continuous jazz festival in the world.

California has so many seasonal festivals and special events that we need a special publication in which to list them all! *California Happenings* magazine makes festival finding fun and easy.

A Rose Colored Parade

Each New Year's Day, the world focuses its attention on Pasadena, home of the Tournament of Roses Parade and Rose Bowl Game. It is a celebration that is more than one hundred years old, a festival of flowers, music, and sports unequaled anywhere else in the world. The Tournament is more than just a parade and a football game. It is a greeting to the world on the first day of the year, a salute to community spirit and a love of pageantry that have thrived in Pasadena for over a century. The Rose Parade is America's kick off to celebrate the New Year!

The Delta

FROM SACRAMENTO, the Sacramento River meanders toward the San Francisco Bay, creating a watery world of islands and sloughs punctuated here and there by a town that looks like the Deep South in the 1950s.

To really experience the charm and culture of the Delta, you're best bet is to have a boat and several days at your disposal. If you can't manage that, you can get a feel for it with a drive down Highway 160, which follows the levees through the often foggy scenes of drawbridges, swing bridges, fruit orchards, and Victorian farmhouses.

A highlight of any Delta trip, especially for photographers, is the tiny town of Locke, the first community in the United States built solely by Chinese for Chinese. Its sagging, weathered wooden buildings today house, among other things, a Chinese grocery store that does a big business selling egg rolls to Spanish-speaking farmworkers. Now that's California!

The Delta is also known as a fisherman's haven. If the yearning to throw a line in the water becomes impossible to resist, head to Bethel Island, one of fifty-five islands in the Delta, where you can rent a boat and sightsee as you troll for striped bass, blue gill, black bass, or, during the fall spawning season, salmon and steelhead trout.

A recent UC Berkeley report reveals that the typical Delta fisher prefers boating, viewing the wildlife, and enjoying scenery to visiting historical or cultural sites.

San Diego's Beach Scene

Southern California, one-third of the entire state, is home to one-half of the state's thirty-two and a half million residents. Ninety percent of those live within one hundred miles of the beach. There are seventy-six miles of shoreline in San Diego County, where many coastal locals live the quintessential Southern California beach lifestyle. One of the world's most popular TV shows *Baywatch* has been Los Angeles-based, but in San Diego, you *turn off* your TV and go outside—where life really is a beach.

★ ★ ★

Hacky-sack: The Solitaire of the beach games. This game consists of keeping a little leather ball up in the air with your feet. Sometimes you'll see it played in groups, but usually it's played solo, good for passing time, as in, when you don't have anything better to do.

Mission Beach and Mission Bay are two opposing beach lifestyles in one beach town and both, depending on your mood, are appealing.

MISSION BEACH—Ocean Front Walk is three miles of paved insanity. In true Southern California style, swarms of sun worshipers speed in opposite directions on bikes, rollerblades, and skateboards, some of which are pulled by dogs. At the end of Ocean Front Walk is Belmont Park, an amusement park and shopping center, home to the "Giant Dipper," a red, white, and blue, seventy-three-year-old rollercoaster.

MISSION BAY—The peninsula of Mission Bay is quiet and therefore very different from the atmosphere at the beach just a kite flight away. Bay Side Walk is a three-mile, paved, winding road. It runs between the bay and a narrow strip of beach that is dotted with volleyball nets, catamarans, and American flags. The other side of the walk is lined with a charming assortment of homes, each with perfectly manicured, pint-sized portions of grass, on which families barbecue and play badminton. The pace along the walk is leisurely. Between the two, Mission Beach and Mission Bay epitomize the Southern California beach scene.

La Jolla, which means "the jewel" in Spanish. Legendary waves and a sandy, flat beach front a gorgeous village with ultra-sophisticated shopping and great restaurants.

And they're off! "Where the Surf Meets the Turf" at Del Mar Racetrack. Take your money, wear your lucky socks, and have a good time! The thoroughbreds race a forty-three-day season beginning in late July.

Carlsbad is a village by the sea. South Carlsbad State Beach is best for surfing. Pebbles and rocks cover some of the beaches now so they aren't what they used to be, but spa living is better than ever. La Costa Resort & Spa, in Carlsbad, is a world-class golf and tennis resort. Be sure to visit Carlsbad's latest fun-filled attraction, Legoland.

For a different kind of inspiration, visit the Self-Realization Fellowship Retreat, Gardens, and Hermitage in Encinitas. You can't miss it; the lotus flower towers stand out like a beacon on Highway 101. This seventeen-acre place of worship was founded in 1937 by Paramahansa Yogananda and built cliffside in 1938. His *Autobiography of a Yogi* is a spiritual classic, as is this beautiful site to which visitors from all walks of life are always welcome.

Castles and Mansions

Touring the opulent castles and mansions of California is a way to get a vicarious thrill and a close-up look at how the very rich, and sometimes famous, live or used to live. By walking through the castle doors or across the mansion grounds, a lot can be learned about the people who lived in them as well as about California history. Driving tours are offered around some and walking tours through others. The tours provide useful information about these great homes, but even the tours leave you wishing the walls could talk.

★   ★   ★

When you're talking castles, few places on earth compare to Hearst Castle in San Simeon. William Randolph Hearst built the 165-room castle (surrounded by sixty thousand acres of land) five tons at a time, by the wagonload. Hearst purchased priceless tapestries, carpets, furnishings, and art from grand old estates in Europe after World War I. There is even a gold-plated swimming pool. Hearst Castle is the second-most popular sightseeing attraction in California, surpassed only by Disneyland.

In the late 1800s, Victorian homes came into vogue and were built in San Francisco and other northern cities where redwood lumber was readily available. The Queen Anne-style Carson Mansion in Eureka is one of the most picturesque with its high chimneys, bulging bay windows, towers, and turrets.

The Wrigley Mansion on Santa Catalina Island was built as a vacation home by the chewing gum tycoon. It is now an exclusive bed and breakfast.

At Hugh Hefner's Playboy Mansion near Beverly Hills, beautiful girls and furry bunnies abound. The English Tudor-style mansion has been home to Hefner since the '60s, and many charity events and pajama parties have been held on the grounds. He hosts his parties lavishly in a way that was lost in the 1920s—Gatsby style. Hef refers to his home as Shangri-La.

Scotty's Castle in Death Valley really belonged to Chicago millionaire Albert Johnson who rarely visited his summer getaway. Scotty was just the housesitter who claimed the huge, neo-Spanish hacienda was the result of his secret gold-mine find.

One of the Big Four, magnate Henry Huntington built his opulent home in San Marino, near Pasadena. Now the Huntington Library Art Collections and the Botanical Gardens, the estate houses forty-nine original Shakespeare folios and quartos, two hundred acres of gardens, and a multimillion-dollar art collection.

The towering spires and minarets of the Winchester Mystery House in San Jose give it a dark aura of mystery. Sarah Winchester was the heiress to the firearm fortune of Winchester Repeating

Arms Company. The pioneers of the nineteenth century considered the Winchester rifle as "the gun that won the West," but Sarah believed the spirits of people killed by her family's guns had placed a curse on her. She was advised by a medium to move West and build a house. As long as the building continued, she was told, the spirits would stay away. Sarah bought an eight-room farmhouse in 1884. It remained under construction for thirty-eight years. When she died in 1922, the house had 160 rooms.

The Migliavacca Mansion in Napa is on the National Register of Historic Places. Giacomo Migliavacca migrated from Italy and settled in Napa in 1867. He opened a small grocery story that was soon known for its fine wine selection. He and his wife had thirteen children and built an impressive three-floor Queen Anne mansion with a gabled roof and stained-glass windows. There are five bedrooms, a ballroom, a coachman's corner, a parlor, a sitting room, and a reception hall. After Giacomo died, his son James became director of the Bank of Italy, which later became the Bank of America. In 1925, the family sold the house. It has been moved twice, vandalized, left in isolation, and restored. It is now divided into seven offices and is located on Fourth Street in Napa.

Alcatraz

THE BARREN SANDSTONE ISLAND in San Francisco Bay, inhabited only by seagulls for thousands of years, made Alcatraz ideally suited to be an escape-proof prison. In 1933, the U.S. government redesigned Alcatraz as a federal penitentiary. It was needed as a "super prison" for "public enemies" such as Al Capone, "Machine Gun" Kelly, Alvin "Creepy" Karpis, and Robert "Birdman" Stroud.

After additions were made to the prison, a secret train was sent out to each maximum security penitentiary in the country—without any advance notice. Incorrigible crooks were loaded on board and headed to San Francisco. Destination: Alcatraz. Though Alcatraz was virtually escape proof, there was one attempt thought possibly to have been successful.

Inmates Frank Morris and John and Clarence Aglin, two brothers, spent their time at night chipping away through the rear walls of their cells. They covered their work with cardboard grates. The men constructed heads of themselves with wire, newspaper, concrete, paint, and human hair. At night, during head count, they fooled the guards by putting the dummy heads in their beds.

On June 12, 1962, the three inmates, obviously willing to risk death rather than remain confined at Alcatraz any longer, climbed up through the utility corridors and the ventilator onto the roof. They headed north to the end of the island and then, on flotation devices they had prepared, slipped into the cold, dark waters and were never seen again. No one knows for sure if they drowned in the freezing dark waters or escaped.

The Golden Gate National Recreation Area maintains Alcatraz today. On March 21, 1963, Attorney General Robert Kennedy officially closed the prison, but the fascination of Alcatraz remains. The Rock's crumbling structure attracts over nine hundred thousand visitors a year.

Gold Trails and Ghost Towns

WHEN JOHN MARSHALL discovered gold on the South Fork of the American River in El Dorado County ("the land of the gilded man"), the stampede to Cal-i-for-ni-ay began. As a result, Mother Lode country developed. The nine counties that make up the Mother Lode are Amador, Calaveras, El Dorado, Mariposa, Nevada, Placer, Tuolumne, Sierra, and Yuba. "Going to see the elephant" was a term used during the gold rush years by those who dreamed of the instant wealth that finding gold in California's earth could provide.

Those days are gone, but the longing to recapture the high-drama, outlaw, gold-diggin' days remains, and can be experienced by gold trail and ghost town exploring.

The old mining town of Coulterville in Mariposa County was originally called Banderita (little flag) and is one of the most picturesque and interesting on the Mother Lode. In 1851, the Fandango Hall and Saloon were built and still stand, along with a large "hangman's tree," reputed to have served in sixty hangings. The old Wells Fargo Building was turned into a museum and there is an old locomotive and giant tailing wheels on view.

The town of Columbia in Tuolumne County originated in 1850. In six weeks its population grew to six thousand and kept growing until it reached its peak at twenty thousand. There were forty saloons and twenty-seven general stores in this once-bustling town. Still standing and well-preserved today are many buildings, including the Wells Fargo Office, some saloons and firehouses, and the Masonic Temple.

Settled in 1850 by lawless miners, Horintos (little ovens) in Mariposa County was considered one of the wildest towns of all, where $44,000 worth of gold a day was shipped out from the first Wells Fargo office in the county. Some of the old buildings from the town are still in use, including the jail.

Bodie State Historical Park in the Sierra Nevada is the most picturesque ghost town in California. Although it has been ravaged by fire many times over, many buildings such as the firehouse, saloon, livery stable, and miners' union hall are still standing. Bodie was a mining town and the site of many stage holdups, and therefore, it has become legendary to ghost town addicts. In its heydey the population was ten thousand. You can drive the thirteen miles of road from Highway 395 into Bodie, then walk through town.

Panamint City in Inyo County came up in 1873 when silver deposits were discovered. It boomed into a rough, lawless town and then was devastated in 1876 by a flash flood. You'll need an off-road vehicle to drive up Surprise Canyon to get to the site of the Panamint City ghost town.

If you love the gold rush era, then Old Sacramento, near the state capitol, might be the place for you. Although it's not a ghost town it is a twenty-eight-acre national historic landmark, featuring over one hundred gold rush-era sites, including an ornate theater built in 1849, a schoolhouse, and the California State Railroad Museum.

STAR TRACKING

I was pretty cocky in the early '8os when I was twenty years old. I was living in New York City in my brother's apartment while he was in Los Angeles pursuing his television acting career for the summer. My brother persuaded me to come out to L.A. for a week's vacation. When I arrived on the West Coast, I was informed that my brother's old friends, Danny DeVito and Rhea Perlman, were getting married and that we had been invited to the wedding reception up in the Hollywood Hills.

My first Hollywood party! What would I wear? But most importantly, what celebrities would be there? Danny had just finished his television series, Taxi. *That meant that Judd Hirsch might be there; Marilu Henner might be there; but, wait—just a minute—that meant TONY DANZA MIGHT BE THERE! I LOVED TONY DANZA!!!!! I thought he was so handsome, I loved those tight T-shirts he wore on* Taxi, *and I loved his New York accent. Wouldn't it be great if I saw him at the party?*

I arrived at the reception wearing my New York finest. All black— a black Betsey Johnson mini-dress, black fishnet hose, and black Beatle boots. My extremely long wavy hair was caught up into a high ponytail, and I wore big, gold hoop earrings. As I waded through the sea of pastels and white, I realized that the black clothing fad had not yet hit Los Angeles! I began to feel a little self-conscious when someone tapped me on the shoulder. It was Mackenzie Phillips, formerly of One Day at a Time. *"Where do I know you from?" she smiled, wagging her finger at me. I smiled and told her that we had never met. She took a sip of Perrier and paused in thought. "No. We have met. I'll remember it."*

Egad! I had simply wanted to look at celebrities—to observe them. If they were going to talk to me, I would need to bolster my strength. I grabbed a glass of chardonnay off the passing tray and drank thirstily. Where, oh where, was Tony Danza? I just wanted to stand next to him, see how tall he was compared to me, check out the biceps, the hair, the eyes, then I could leave. I felt I was in over my head with this crowd!

With each sip of chardonnay, I grew more and more lively. I danced with Judd Hirsch and then asked him if Tony Danza were coming to the party. He said yes. I began my search mission for Tony in earnest. I went out on the balcony and found John Belushi and Dan Ackroyd but no Tony. Belushi was balancing himself with his stomach on the balcony rail high above a sheer drop. Ackroyd looked on nervously with his hands in his pockets and an uneasy smile on his face. I moved on.

In the sitting room, I found Jack Nicholson holding court, with a glass of scotch or whiskey and a big cigar in his hand. His cronies were also puffing stogies and the air was so gray and thick that I had to look very closely for Tony. But still, no Tony. With a few chardonnays under my belt, I looked at Jack and muttered, "Gawd, it stinks in here!" Jack et al. were not amused.

Finally, defeated, I returned to the main room. I grabbed one last chardonnay when I spied Mackezie Phillips working her way across the room to me. Oh, no! I don't know her! She doesn't believe me! Help! I began to work my way through the tightly knit crowd, when suddenly I was heavily jostled from behind. Wobbling and struggling to stay upright and not drop my wine glass on the snowy white carpet, I felt myself in a perfect tango dip position with one leg bent up in the air, back supported, and my long pony-

tail gracefully brushing the floor. What miracle was this? Perhaps I had fainted and I was dreaming. But no, I felt strong arms holding me and warm breath on my face. I opened my eyes to stare right into the big, brown eyes of TONY DANZA!

"I am so sorry. Ohmigosh, are you okay? I bumped you so hard. Are you okay?" Tony pleaded. I could only shake my head up and down. I was speechless. Tony stood me upright and held onto my hand. "Are you sure? I guess I'm a little tipsy and I was moving my hands around too much." Tony continued to look intently into my face. I still couldn't speak. "Well, I guess you'll survive. Be careful and watch out for me!" Tony grinned, squeezed my hand, and walked away.

For the rest of the evening, whenever Tony saw me, he would point at me and give me the thumbs up. If he passed by me, he would pat my shoulder. Jack looked at me with new curiosity. Mackenzie nodded in approval. It was evident to everyone at the party that me and Tony knew each other. Who was this fascinating creature in black that had Tony Danza's eye?

Oh, yeah. It was obvious to everyone. Me and Tony Danza, we had a thing.

KATE EDWARDS, Santa Monica

RANDOM FUN STUFF

Shasta Lake is the houseboat capital of the west. There are thirty thousand surface acres and 370 miles of shoreline that make it California's largest lake and one of America's most diversified outdoor sports areas.

Bassmaster Magazine rated Lake Oroville in Butte County "the best fishing spot in California."

Fresno is the only city in the nation just ninety minutes from three national parks: Yosemite, Kings Canyon, and Sequoia. On your way to Yosemite, on Highway 41, stop and pan for gold at Coarsegold Creek. Just ask fer "Gabby," the Coarsegold Prospector.

FYI: Kings Canyon National Park is deeper than the Grand Canyon.

Shop till you drop. Like it or not, right or wrong, it's what we do. Shopping has become sport, a way of life, and a way to pass time. California is an affluent state, and this is never more apparent than when strolling in any of our one hundred major malls. That may not sound like a lot until you stop and consider how big each mall is. For example, the largest is the Great Mall of the Bay Area in Milpitas. It is the equivalent of fifty-two football fields. South Coast Plaza in Costa Mesa has nearly three hundred stores. The greater Los Angeles area has the most major malls. But there's a lot more to do at the mall than just shop. We can accomplish nearly everything on our list with one mall stop. With movie complexes and food/video courts, malls have become a favorite hangout for kids. They are a place where we can all get out of the heat or come in out of the cold. It's even a way to get a little relief from singing the blues. Fashion Valley Shopping Center in San Diego, with 129 stores, is the largest revenue producing mall in the nation! Any way you cut it, there's a whole lot of shopping goin' on.

Take a guess at how many historical landmarks there are in California. If you guessed 1,070 you were right.

If you're ever in San Luis Obispo, check out the Madonna Inn. When walking through this thirty-five-year-old landmark you have to wonder, what were they thinking? Each of the 109 rooms is uniquely decorated. The main building is built in several different architectures of the world and the inside is, well, imaginative to say the least.

The Tehama County Fairgrounds in Red Bluff, hosts the largest three-day rodeo in the U.S.

Coffeehouses have become the bars of the day. Society lingers over lattes and delves into intense conversations after a couple of cappuccinos. Designer coffee drinks made up of your favorite grind, and even plain coffee, can be found in thousands of coffee bars across the state. In Silicon Valley alone there are over eighty. Seems the caffeine of the coffee bean is the popular buzz of the day.

On the slopes of the Plumas Eureka Ski Bowl in Johnsville, history comes alive with the longboard ski revival series races. Every year in Janurary, February, and March, the races commemorate the first recorded ski racing in the western hemisphere. The place, Plumas County. The year, 1860. Move aside because racers compete on thirteen-foot-long wooden skis with leather bindings, using home-made wax and a single wooden pole for stopping. Period costumes and other 1800s traditions, music, and food are all part of the fun.

Of all the fun things to do in San Francisco, riding the cable car is that extra dash of flavor in our most European town. This cog-wheel system was the brainchild of English engineer Andrew Halli-die and was brought into use in 1873.

Skateboarding is big and it's bad. And don't call it sidewalk surfing. Skateboarding has become one of the fastest growing sports in the nation, right up there with snowboarding. Actually, skateboarding has been around a long time. It's all the cool tricks that are new.

THE TIME I LEARNED HOW TO OLLIE

I started skateboarding when I was about eleven, with a cheap skateboard that cost around $30. Before you can learn any tricks, you have to know the basic trick of all—it's called the "ollie." The ollie is a trick that involves getting somewhat off the ground by jumping with the skateboard into the air. At the time, that was the trick I was trying to learn. It took me about two or three weeks before I learned how to do an ollie.

It was a hot summer day. I was out in front of my porch trying to do this ollie, when all of a sudden I did it! I had ollied for the first time! It was the greatest feeling I had ever felt in my life. I couldn't feel my legs and I was overwhelmed. So then I tried to ollie one more time (thinking I wouldn't be able to do it), but I did it again and again and again. Finally after weeks of hard work, I had learned how to ollie.

After that, I felt like I was on top of the world. But now I look back on that day and think, "Big wow. An ollie, how hard is that?" Right now an ollie to me is pretty much just a basic trick, but it's still a trick and an important one too.

EMILIO RAMOS, Alhambra

Arts and Education

CALIFORNIA'S EDUCATION has been molded and shaped as interest in our land has increased and ownership over it changed.

Long ago, before the Spanish claimed California as theirs, the Indians who inhabited this land were taught how to live in the wilderness and in harmony with nature. The culture was strongly matriarchal, where the squaw taught, through informal apprenticeship and oral tradition, tribal tongue, legends, and basketry. The teachings were by word of mouth. Young braves learned the arts of hunting, fishing, dancing, and weapon and war making. Each generation passed on a respect of nature and the techniques of living in harmony with and surviving in nature. This is the essence of Indian education.

In 1769, the Portolá Party sailed through the Presidio of San Francisco, led by Spaniard Father Serra on his "Sacred Expedition." Within three years Father Serra had begun to colonize California, establishing the first nine missions, which represented the most outstanding Spanish educational efforts in California.

Struggles over California's ownership continued between Spain and Mexico. Pio Pico, the last Mexican governor, and previous *alcaldes* had done quite a lot to promote reasonably good education by requiring parents to send their children to school and to pay taxes where schools existed.

During the 1840s, increasing numbers of newcomers from the United States arrived and settled in California. They brought with them their educational values, including a high regard for mass literacy and civility, along with experience in the state system of schooling and in social institutions. And then in 1848, with the discovery of gold, people came by wagon- and boatload from all over the world, and California was admitted into statehood, becoming the thirty-first state in 1850.

The foundations of California's school system were laid down by forty-eight delegates from widely different backgrounds, cultures, interests, and training. Seven were Mexican Californians, five were European, and the remaining thrity-six were delegates from thirteen of the thirty states. The state constitutional convention met from September 1 to October 13, 1849, in Colton Hall at Monterey. The final draft of California's first constitution outlined the state government in twelve articles. Article IX was Education (the California school system).

The first public schools were in San Francisco, and demands during the 1850s were greater than the new system could accommodate. Soon students in smaller towns nearby were following San Francisco's lead. In 1854, Californians were supporting a total of forty-seven schools in San Francisco and surrounding areas.

Those early planners dreamed of cultivating an institution of higher learning that would "encourage by all suitable means the promotion of intellectual, scientific, moral and agricultural improvement." The seeds were planted. The infancy stages of the state's first college, the College of California, began in 1849, took root, and today is known as UC Berkeley.

"The children of California shall be our children" was the real beginning of Stanford University. Leland Stanford, one of the Big Four, and his wife, Jane Lathrop, lost their only child to typhoid fever. On October 1, 1891, after six years of planning, Stanford University opened its doors.

Today there are 456 colleges and universities in California, several of which have many thousands of students. Add to that another 1,600 types of programs that lead to degrees, certificates, or credentials. Available among them are internationally recognized traditional institutions as well as a wide assortment of alternative education opportunities. These are big numbers when you compare them to the 599 colleges and universities in the twelve states of the Midwest.

Many of our schools foster the arts and artists. People impassioned by a creative force commonly move to California. Why? Because there are only a few communities in the world that are not threatened by original thought, and California is one of them.

Doing something differently often requires doing it first, which challenges the status quo. Walking to the beat of a different drummer very often results in being the square peg that doesn't fit in the round hole. Only one of the unusual characteristics that makes California so unique is its attraction to so many creative people. Not only is the brainchild of invention more acceptable here, it is encouraged and nurtured in our schools.

California is a fertile ground where art is a way of life, and new ways of doing things can blossom into fruition. If you underestimate the power of imagination and the vision of a creative few, consider the driving force behind Hollywood, the people who dared to think differently in the Silicon Valley, and the radical new thought of a generation that sprang out of Berkeley in the 1960s, forever changing the direction of the world.

Creativity is one of this state's greatest resources. So write it down, whisper it to the wind, shout it from across the stage. California has artists tucked away in every corner, changing the world one idea, one dance step, one stroke, and one written word at a time.

Father of Silicon Valley

LONG AGO FREDERICK TERMAN, Stanford's famous professor of electrical engineering, dean, and later provost, was the first to envision integrating academics, government, and industrial engineering between Stanford and the Silicon Valley. And then he trained many of the students who made it happen.

Frederick Terman was the son of Lewis Terman, the celebrated Stanford psychologist, so Frederick literally grew up on campus. Later, when he became a student at Stanford himself, his focus was electrical engineering. The chairman of the electrical engineering department at Stanford at the time told Terman that MIT had the best electrical engineering department in the country. And so, in 1922, Terman went to check it out. What he learned was this: MIT's strength was due to the successful relationship they had developed and nurtured off the campus with the electrical business community.

In 1926, Terman brought that and other invaluable information back home and put it to work at Stanford. In 1934, Terman, who would become known as the "father of Silicon Valley," helped Stanford students William Hewlett and David Packard go into business together. Their original Palo Alto garage address has been named the "birthplace of the Silicon Valley."

Stanford University Preps Silicon Valley

STANFORD AND SILICON VALLEY go together like monitors and keyboards. Between Stanford and surrounding areas, there has been a longstanding flow of people and information supporting business in the Silicon Valley—and far outside it. At Stanford, people who would not usually work together, either because they came from different academic disciplines or they worked at different companies, work shoulder to shoulder. Students, faculty, corporate scientists, and engineers sharing the same interests come together and combine their strengths in a technical interchange on campus.

More than 350 technology-based companies have been founded by members of the Stanford community. Among them are:

Hewlett-Packard Company

Amati Communications Group

IDEO

Cypress Semiconductor

Of all the university campuses, Stanford houses one of the most extensive computer environments. SUNnet, Stanford University Network, connects thirty-five thousand host computers. About six gigabytes of data per day is transferred onto the Internet from Stanford via Web requests! If you're not sure what a giga is, it's a mere one thousand million. Additional companies are:

Yahoo! Inc.

Intuit, Inc.

MIPS Technologies, Inc.

SRI International

Work-study programs at Stanford select twelve highly motivated computer science seniors per year to work for the summer at the hottest high-tech, fast-growth Silicon Valley companies. During their internships, the companies agree to spend plenty of time supervising students and to pay them a competitive wage. These companies include:

Cisco Systems

Junglee

Excite, Inc.

Trilogy

Four women and six men were chosen in the program's first year. Instead of spending the summer around the Bay or at the beach, the students took jobs ranging from circuit design and low-level engineering to strategic planning. During the following fall quarter, the students prepare formal presentations about their on-the-job experience, which is then presented to their group and their company bosses, who are required to be in attendance. Other companies are:

3Com Corporation

Rambus, Inc.

Varian Associates, Inc.

Cynthia Yu, twenty-three, while interning at MMC Networks in Sunnyvale, is already talking about paying off the bulky debt she has accrued as a Stanford student. She received stock options while working for the company and after graduating, when she goes to work with the company full time, she expects to get more. More companies are:

Octel Communications Corporation

Pure Software, Inc.

Tandem Computers, Inc.

The entrepreneurial internship program is such a success that each of the students receives multiple summer job offers. Tom Byers, Stanford's associate professor of engineering, had to put a limit on the number of students any one firm could hire. In addition to on-the-job experience, prominent Silicon Valley figures come to Stanford and speak on a regular basis. Everybody benefits!

The Claremont Colleges

"A COLLEGE OF THE NEW ENGLAND TYPE" was created in California in 1887, when Pomona College, the founding member of the Claremont Colleges was built.

The Claremont colleges consist of five undergraduate colleges and one graduate school. In this incomparable consortium exists a major academic community of five thousand students. The colleges are on adjoining campuses in the quaint and lovely town of Claremont. Each is independent, with their own faculty, student body, administration, and circular emphasis ranging from philosophy and religion to science and engineering.

The members of the consortium and their founding dates are: Pomona College (1887), Claremont Graduate University (1925), Claremont McKenna College (1946), Harvey Mudd (1955), and Pitzer College (1963).

The Advanced Surgical Suite for Trauma Casualites. What does it mean? Also known as Hospital in a Box, it was developed by students from Harvey Mudd, San Jose State, and the Army and Marines. Its function is to save the battlefield wounded. This 4,000-pound box is dropped by helicopter and sets up into a medical supplies-filled, 900-square-foot, climate-controlled suite. In less than thirty minutes. Wow!

Campus Trivia

The University of California system is one of the most diverse and internationally renowned state systems in the country. Its diversity and academics earn it a reputation as being one of the best college consortiums in the world. The nine campuses that make up the UC System are Berkeley, Davis, Irvine, Los Angeles, Riverside, San Diego, San Francisco, Santa Barbara, and Santa Cruz. Here is a glimpse at some unusual things you may not know about them.

★　★　★

UC Santa Barbara is bordered on three sides by the Pacific Ocean.

UCLA was the first university in the country to offer a graduate degree in Asian American Studies.

Former Black Panther, Angela Davis, is a professor at UC Santa Cruz.

UC Berkeley has one of the highest numbers of faculty-scholar Nobel laureates per capita in the world.

A professional study showed that UCLA's impact on the national economy exceeds $4 billion.

UC Davis delivers students around campus on red double-decker London buses.

UC San Francisco's School of Pharmacy was established in 1872, the first college of pharmacy in the West.

UC Berkeley is the number one contributor of Peace Corps volunteers of any university in the United States.

The main library at UC San Diego is named after Theodore Geisel, as in Dr. Seuss, who was a long-time resident of La Jolla. Green eggs, anyone?

The UC Berkeley campus is the oldest of the UC campuses, established in 1868. The eucalyptus grove and the oak trees along Strawberry Creek and South Hall link Berkeley to the gold rush days, when the University's first buildings stood alone in orchards.

UC San Diego has no football team. But they have a killer surf team! And there are intramural sports as well. Inner-tube water polo and ultimate Frisbee are favorites.

UC Davis has an insect identification hotline. Should you ever find an unidentified creeper crawling on your person, call them!

Students fight tooth and claw to get into Davis School of Veterinary Medicine; the only such school in California, it is ranked first nationally in its field.

The Medical Center at UCLA, with more than twenty miles of corridor, is one of the largest buildings in the world.

The campus at UC San Diego has a movie theater.

UCLA sport teams are second in the nation in the total number of NCAA championships won. *Sports Illustrated* rated it the number one "jock school."

A popular weekend jaunt for UC San Diego students is to cross the border into Tijuana for a taco-filled Corona blast.

The minority population at UC Irvine is 77 percent.

UCLA has the highest enrollment of the UC campuses.

One of the clubs at UC San Diego is RISC. That's for Radically Inclined Ski Club, for those of you out of the know.

There are between 15,000 to 18,000 bikes traveling the UC Davis campus daily. Tickets are issued for cycling under the influence and for speeding. Fifteen miles an hour is the speed limit. The students at UC Davis say their unofficial campus mascot should be the bike.

The biggest game of the year at Berkeley is the Berkeley/Stanford football game. Months before the game, Berkeley students start chanting "Take off that red shirt," their archrival's school color.

UC Santa Cruz has no football team, and they don't want one.

Approximately 42,000 students each year graduate from UC's nine campuses, including 10 percent of the nation's PhD's. More than one million degrees have been awarded.

Coach John Wooden

IT'S PRETTY MUCH A GIVEN that John Robert Wooden, with twenty-seven UCLA seasons and winner of ten NCAA championships, is college basketball's finest coach.

Wooden began his basketball career in Indiana where he was All-American at Purdue in 1930. Before he arrived at UCLA in 1948, the basketball team was not very well known. The Bruins started making noise though, when in 1964, they managed thirty consecutive wins. Wooden's team that year had an average height of six-foot-five. Part of his winning equation was that in the last minutes of the game, Wooden expected his team to outrun their opponents. Another was that he stressed conditioning and fundamentals. Between 1971 and 1974, with seven-foot Lew Alcindor (who went on to the NBA as Kareem Abdul-Jabbar) and six-foot-eleven Bill Walton, the Bruins reeled off eighty-eight consecutive wins—the longest winning streak in the history of college basketball.

Wooden believed that clean living and fair playing were basic principles in competitive greatness—something he knew of firsthand. When he retired in 1975, after UCLA won its tenth NCAA title, he became the only person ever inducted into the National Basketball Hall of Fame as both a coach and a player.

Aggies

UC Davis has emerged as an acknowledged international leader in agricultural, biological, biotechnological, and environmental sciences—which is saying a lot. Don't think California and agriculture go together? Our Great Central Valley, a mere 430 miles long, is the richest farming region in the world. And Davis is right out there in the middle of it all, getting their hands dirty with the best of them.

More than 155 new varieties of fruits, vegetables, and grains have sprung from Davis agricultural research.

California's internationally renowned wine industry owes much of its success to Davis. Scientists have assisted it in understanding growing climates and developing new grape varieties.

Davis has committed to a one-hundred-year research project devoted to studies about agriculture and its impact on the environment.

The once medical technique for testing toxic contamination in food has been made faster, cheaper, and more convenient by Davis scientists. Pesticides, pollutants, and recombinant DNA are identified.

The development of new farm machinery and crops adapted to their use by Davis engineers has helped revolutionize California's agricultural industry. One invention is a special tomato for machine harvesting.

Take a guess at how many varieties of tomatoes there might be. Davis has over three thousand in their Tomato Genetics Resource Center.

Up the creek without a fin. Biologists at Davis have found that a high number of California's native fish species are seriously threatened. One of the principal causes is the introduction of nonnative species.

Do you know what the Williamson Act is? It is the state legislation aimed at helping to preserve agricultural land and provide tax relief to farmers. Work by UC Davis scholars proved instrumental in its development and subsequent revisions.

Another fish story. Due to overfishing, sturgeon are now being raised in fish farms because of their greatly reduced numbers. Davis researchers played a major role in developing methods for commercial sturgeon farming.

Some Nobel Prize Winners

UC BERKELEY

Ernest O. Lawrence	1939	*Physics*
Glenn T. Seaborg	1951	*Chemistry*
Edwin M. McMillan	1951	*Chemistry*
John Steinbeck	1962	*Literature*
Luis W. Alvarez	1966	*Physics*
Czeslaw Milosz	1980	*Literature*
John Harsanyi	1994	*Economics*

STANFORD

Felix Bloch	1952	*Physics*
Kenneth J. Arrow	1972	*Economics*
Paul Berg	1980	*Chemistry*
Gary S. Becker	1992	*Economics*
Steven Chu	1997	*Physics*
Robert B. Laughlin	1998	*Physics*

UC SAN DIEGO

Francis Crick	1962	*Chemistry*
Maria Goeppert-Mayer	1963	*Physics*
Susumu Tonegawa	1987	*Medicine*

CALTECH

Robert A. Millikan	1923	*Physics*
Linus Pauling	1954	*Chemistry*
Linus Pauling	1962	*Peace*
David Baltimore	1975	*Medicine*
Edward Lewis	1995	*Physiology*
Robert C. Merton	1997	*Economics*

UCLA

Julian Schwinger	1965	*Physics*
Donald J. Cram	1987	*Chemistry*
Louis J. Ingnarro	1998	*Medicine*

UC IRVINE

Frederick Reines	1995	*Physics*
Sherwood Rowland	1995	*Chemistry*

UC SANTA BARBARA

Robert Schrieffer	1972	*Physics*
Walter Kohn	1998	*Chemistry*

UC SAN FRANCISCO

J. Michael Bishop	1989	*Medicine*
Harold Varmus	1989	*Medicine*

The Big Time

In the sixties, turbulent times rocked the world and the most historic event of the century would take place: man would walk on the moon. America went to war against communism in Vietnam and Cambodia. California native, Vice President Richard Nixon, was busy representing America all over the world trying to put those communist fires out. For many of the love generation, Nixon's rise to president in 1969 was a bitter pill to swallow.

Richard Milhouse Nixon was born in a small farmhouse in Yorba Linda and raised in Whittier. He attended Whittier High School, where, as a junior, he decided to study law and become a politician. He went on to Whittier College where he graduated second in his class in 1934. In 1937, Nixon graduated with honors from Duke University Law School. He returned to his hometown of Whittier where he joined a law firm. He met his future wife, Pat, who was raised on a farm in Artesia, put herself through USC, graduated with honors, and moved to Whittier, where she worked as a teacher. They were married in 1940. In 1947, Whittier's first citizen was elected to Congress. In 1951, at age thirty-eight, Richard Nixon was the youngest member in the United States Senate. One year later, Nixon became General Eisenhower's running mate and was swept into the second highest office in the land, Vice President. In January 1969, Richard Nixon took the oath of office as thirty-seventh President of the United States. On August 9, 1974, he resigned the Presidency under the dark cloud of the Watergate break-in and subsequent cover up.

Neil Alden Armstrong received his Master of Science degree in Aerospace Engineering from the University of Southern California. In 1962, he was accepted by NASA as an astronaut. On July 16, 1969, Apollo 11 began their trip to the moon.

Summer of Love

THERE WAS SOMETHING HAPPENING in San Francisco. A generation was speaking its mind, and its voice was being heard through the music. On the campuses of Stanford and Berkeley, the stand for free love was falling into the center of a revolution. Vice President Nixon lost the presidential race to John F. Kennedy, who was assassinated in 1963. Lyndon Johnson was elected, and America became even more deeply involved in the Vietnam War. In 1968, Reverend Martin Luther King Jr. was gunned down in Memphis, and Senator Robert Kennedy was shot in Los Angeles. Segregation in the South continued, and riots erupted around the country. Mistrust and resentment reached new heights as the number of American soldiers in Vietnam reached an all-time high. Richard Nixon was elected president in 1969.

In the 1960s, the American campus came alive. The hotbed of activity was on the campus of UC Berkeley with antiwar protests and the Free Speech Movement sit-in of 1964. The FSM was the first time that students focused their attacks on the administration; the "system" was regarded as the oppressor and denier of rights. Their protest against the establishment shook across California campuses, creating many aftershocks.

In the winter of 1965, a two-day antiwar protest began on the Berkeley campus with a garbled harmonica version of "Home on the Range." Joe McDonald, who had been in the Navy in Japan, and his partner Barry Melton of Country Joe and the Fish, sang on campus from the back of a flatbed truck:

And it's 1 . . . 2 . . . 3 . . .
What are we fighting for?
Don't ask me I don't give a damn
Next stop is Vietnam

The Hells Angels roaring into Berkeley could be heard before they were seen. The peace rally ended in an all-out battle off campus with the bikers beating the protesters and the police beating the bikers. Cops were taken to the hospital and the Angels were taken to jail. But Country Joe's lyrics struck a chord; all over Berkeley, Oakland, and San Francisco the tune became an anthem of antiwar protest.

LSD was being tested on the Stanford campus. It was not yet illegal, and the first public acid test took place on December 4, 1965, at someone's house in San Jose. Writer Ken Kesey passed around leaflets that read, "Can YOU pass the Acid Test?"

On the peninsula south of San Francisco in Palo Alto, a gentle-souled bohemian named Jerry Garcia taught guitar and played banjo with a band called the Warlocks. Their bluegrass, jug-band music was a fast-growing addition to the San Francisco sound; its whooshing roar made the perfect house music for Kesey's psychedelic scene. Garcia, also fondly referred to as Captain Trips, renamed the band The Grateful Dead.

The intense excitement of the San Francisco scene was peaking and ushered in a liberated age of experimentation, free love, and drug taking—all to music unlike any had heard before. The epicenter of the psychedelic apocalypse was 710 Ashbury, a communal residence near the corner of Haight Street and home of The Grateful Dead.

A young girl named Grace, from a wealthy Pasadena family, saw The Grateful Dead perform one night at the Fillmore, and like many her life was changed. Grace Slick would later leave her band, the Great Society, and join the Jefferson Airplane. Other California bands, called "existencialistas," at the forefront of the San Francisco sound were the Charlatans, Janis Joplin with Big Brother and the Holding Company, Quicksilver Messenger Service, Moby Grape, and Santana. Mystery Trend and the Final Solution were bands mostly made up of San Francisco State students, and The Fifth Dimension added California soul. At the forefront of the California folk-rock bands were The Byrds, Buffalo Springfield, Sonny and Cher, and the Mamas and the Papas. Haight and Ashbury were the crossroads that brought musicians together from all over the world: Jimmy Hendrix, Otis Redding, Bob Dylan, Donovan, the Beatles, the Animals, and the Rolling Stones—they all came.

The summer of love had turned into the winter of discontent, and after the smoke had cleared it was hard to know who had won. For a few minutes though, the world, battered and scarred by division, was brought together again in the final year of the sixties. In July 1969, the spacecraft Apollo 11 turned its camera toward home and five hundred million people from planet Earth saw their world as they had never seen it before. From the Oval Office in the White House, President of the United States, California native, Richard Nixon made the most historic telephone call ever made. He reached the moon and spoke to California-educated Neil Armstrong. The American flag and instruments were deployed along with the plaque that reads:

"Here men from planet Earth first set foot upon the moon.
July 1969 A.D. We came in peace for all mankind."

SOD OR CRABGRASS?

I went to San Francisco for a week in the summer of 1965 to see what was going on. I was seventeen and my friend Ed was sixteen. I remember standing on the corner of Haight and Ashbury. Everybody had long hair. I remember music. Hippie music. People walking by and asking me if I wanted some grass. I asked them if they had sod or crab. I remember Black Panthers and Hells Angels. There was a funeral procession and about five hundred Angels roared into town. It scared the crap out of us. I remember it was hot, and people were driving down the street in cars with their windows rolled up and their doors locked. I remember free speech out in the parks. People were able to take their political stance and publicly talk about it. We went to the Fillmore. We sat on a gymnasium floor while strobe lights flashed and bubbles burped on the wall. Where did we sleep? People were sleeping on benches with newspaper over them for blankets. That was just normal stuff. We just laid down in the park a couple of times for a nap in the middle of the day with everybody else. We didn't really sleep that week.

TONY COLSON, La Costa

An Education in
Alternative Medicine

"East is East and West is West and never the twain shall meet." Never say never. Western education and medicine are being practiced in China today. California was the first state in the nation to offer education in acupuncture where today over four thousand acupuncturists are licensed.

In addition, homeopathic and chiropractic schools are slowly merging with traditional schools of thought. The one thing they all have in common is they all want to help.

There is a lot going on outside the traditional institutions, some of it very valuable, some of it way out there; the point is—California offers a choice! There is such a large selection of alternative education available in California that every student can find their niche. The California spirit is independent, and much of it starts at school.

★　★　★

Mueller College of Holistic Studies in San Diego, which started in 1976, was the first school in the state and the fourteenth in the country to receive curriculum approval from the American Massage Therapy Association. It is a three-year program. There are seven accredited massage therapy schools within the state.

There is a lot to be learned besides Ylang Ylang in the three-year program offered at Michael Scholes School for Aromatherapy studies in Los Angeles.

Acupuncture traces its origins back to the reign of the Yellow Emperor, Huang-ti, 2595 B.C. So it's taken us awhile to catch on— out of the twenty-seven accredited schools of acupuncture and Chinese medicine in the United States today, twelve are in California. Most of them are three- to four-year programs.

Samra University of Oriental Medicine in Los Angeles was the first acupuncture school in the state to be approved by the State Medical Board. It was first authorized by the State Department of Education to grant masters degrees in Oriental medicine in 1979.

American College of Traditional Chinese Medicine in San Francisco has a study abroad program with Goto College of Medical Arts and Sciences in Tokyo. They have worked with San Francisco's Department of Public Health to provide medical care for people with AIDS by using acupuncture and herbal medicines.

In Santa Cruz there are five branches of the Institute College of Traditional Chinese Medicine.

Looking for an education in natural health care? In addition to the accredited institutions listed above, there are several chiropractic, Yoga/Ayurvedic, homeopathic, osteopathic, hypnotherapy, midwifery, and visualization medical institutions in the state.

ANOTHER HAPPY PATIENT

After a nasty break to my tailbone, or coccyx, and living in chronic pain to the point that it was becoming debilitating, I tried acupuncture. After listening to my friend Kelly plead with me to go see her acupuncturist before I underwent yet another surgery, I agreed.

The reason I hesitated for so long was that I could not imagine how such a gentle procedure could correct such a severe problem. After two surgeries, twenty or so doctors appointments, a bone scan, an MRI, dozens of X-rays, sitting on a "donut" pillow for two years, countless massages and saltbaths, potions, creams, and enough medication to choke a horse, out of sheer desperation, I tried acupuncture.

It worked! I consider it a miracle. I have to go once a week, but it is so good for my overall health that I consider it part of my weekly workout and routine. It was my "western" way of thinking that kept me resistant for so long. If it's not invasive, how can it be any good? I realize now just how backward that thinking is.

I am grateful to my friend Kelly who patiently kept at me and to all the gentle people at Yo San University and Clinic. It's just been a miracle in my life.

BOB JONES, Placerville

CAL STATE RULES!

THE CALIFORNIA STATE UNIVERSITY is the largest university system in the Americas. Over 350,000 students are enrolled in its institutions. San Jose was the location for the first public institution of higher learning. In 1857 San Jose State College was first called a "normal school." Over the next century, normal schools became "teachers colleges" and then "state colleges" that were governed by the State Board of Education. In 1960 the Legislature organized them under their own board of trustees into the California State College System. In 1981 it was given its current name.

Here are the CSU campuses (no preferences, the list is alphabetical):

Bakersfield, Channel Islands, Chico, Coachella Valley, Contra Costa, Dominguez Hills, Fresno, Fullerton, Hayward, Humboldt, Imperial Valley, Long Beach, Los Angeles, Maritime Academy, Mission Viejo, Monterey Bay, Northridge, Pomona, Sacramento, San Bernardino, San Diego, San Jose, San Francisco, San Francisco Downtown, San Luis Obispo, San Marcos, Sonoma, and Stanislaus.

It's safe to assume that a lot of people are getting an education in California when you look at these interesting numbers.

California has ninety-seven private colleges, many of which are considered the best in the country.

Community colleges: 106 with a total of over one million enrolled students.

Professional education programs: With thirty-one engineering programs offered in the state, this number is by far the highest offered in the country. In addition California offers the highest number of art and design programs at twenty-eight (New York has twenty), twenty-seven business administration programs (New York has eighteen), and seventeen law programs (New York fifteen). There are thirty-two music, twenty-five culinary, nineteen theology, seventeen psychology, nine journalism and mass communications, and eight architecture institutions in California.

MASCOTS

SCHOOL MASCOTS are usually pretty tame. You will find a lot of horse-type mascots (mustangs and broncos in particular), plenty of fierce cats (wild in particular), and you can count on your average run of bears and warrior types. But here is a look at a few of the more unusual school mascots.

Monterey Bay State is represented by the mighty Otter. (It's an ocean thing.)

The mascot at Pepperdine University in Malibu is King Neptune, whose big, scary head is a papier-mâché version of Bob's Big Boy.

UC Irvine is Peter the Anteater. The anteater suit weighs forty pounds.

Whittier College's mascot is a Poet who carries a pen (mightier than the sword) as its weaponry.

The mascot at Pomona-Pitzer College is Cecil the Sage Hen.

But the all-time weirdest mascot goes to UC Santa Cruz. What state other than California would choose a bright yellow, slimy banana slug to proudly represent them? The students' choice for such a lowly creature serves as their statement regarding the fierce athletic competition fostered at American universities. The banana slug represents nonaggressiveness, flexibility, and, in true California spirit, an iconoclastic challenge toward the status quo. In spite of this, in 1992 the National Directory of College Athletics named the

Santa Cruz Banana Slug the nation's top mascot, and the same year *Sports Illustrated Magazine* named it the nation's best college nickname. Quentin Tarantino specifically requested the student-designed Slug T-shirt be worn by John Travolta in the last few scenes of *Pulp Fiction*.

SCIENCE ON CAMPUS

THE IMPORTANCE OF RESEARCH to society has never been greater. Federal funds and private industrial grants are provided in support of the field of science, and universities are invigorated by contributing to the community. Here is just a small sampling of how two California colleges are contributing to science and the community at large.

Dawnika Blatter, graduate student of geology and geophysics at Berkeley, works with a furnace that melts rocks. This steel-cased container mimics the pressures and temperatures of volcano sites deep in the earth. Her studies show just how large a role water and carbon dioxide have played in the formation of lavas, which in turn educate us about the Earth's evolution. She has studied with her professor of geology, Ian Carmichael, who has worked at Berkeley for thirty years. Blatter has already assisted in teaching five courses.

From Caltech in the 1940s, a seismologist named Charles Richter devised a scale to measure the amount of energy released by an earthquake. Each whole-number increase on the scale represents ten times the increase in the amount of ground vibration.

Talk about a long flight! In 1996, from Caltech's Jet Propulsion Laboratory, the Mars Global Surveyor began its ten-month flight. The spacecraft's mission is to map the planet for two years, then remain an additional three years to act as a relay station for future spacecraft. Stay tuned for more.

UC Berkeley chemistry professor Richard Mathies works from a chip capable of analyzing ninety-six DNA samples. What's the big deal? The chip is so small he can hold it between two fingers. Not that long ago, it required an entire laboratory to analyze just one DNA sample!

Yesterday the moon, today Mars. The Jet Propulsion Laboratory from Caltech developed the Mars Pathfinder for NASA, and it landed in 1997.

The world of new materials, or "materials science," is about creating new stuff—for example, better artificial joints. In part, this is done by exploiting old materials. Nasreen Chopra, a Berkeley graduate student, works with Berkeley professor of physics, Alex Zettl, searching for structures ten times smaller than a needle in a haystack. Called nanotubes, they are smaller than DNA, yet the skinny cylinders of carbon are theoretically ten times stronger than steel. The buzzword here is "nano," which is a billionth of a meter, or if it's easier for you, think of it as the width of about twelve atoms. Zettl and Chopra are still measuring these new materials. If they prove versatile and strong, they could be the future of electronics, making circuits ten times smaller than today's semiconductors. Chopra says she loves the collaboration between the theory people and the experiment people. And we love that this is happening on our college campuses!

Sixteen elements have been discovered at UC Berkeley.

In 1999, Caltech launched the Mars Polar Lander. It is the first spacecraft to set down near the edge of the southern polar cap of Mars, where it will dig for water and soil samples.

What's the world's best climber? A gecko. Postdoctoral researcher Kellar Autumn of UC Berkeley studies the dynamics of this guy's climbing ability. Professor of Integrative Biology Studies Robert Full and his students show that the running movement between all animals, including we human types, is so similar that each leg of a person can be said to move like two legs of a horse, four of a crab, right on up to forty-four of a centipede. What's the point? These studies of bodies in motion are helpful to cleaning up toxins in the ocean and developing stable vehicles for space exploration.

If there's anybody else out there, Caltech might be the first to find out. *2001: A Space Odyssey* is happening a year early at the Jet Propulsion Lab where, together with NASA, scientists will search for the presence of planets in the year 2000. The large, single telescopes that astronomers have used since Galileo's time have been replaced with telescopes called interferometers. These two ten-meter optical telescopes, the largest in the world, when used in tandem can view things too distant to be detected previously by any other telescope. They are separated by the length of a football field! In the year 2010, with a one hundred-meter interferometer, scientists will attempt to analyze whether the planets are habitable and check them out for evidence of life. This could also be called spying on your neighbors—but only time will tell.

INSPIRATION + EDUCATION = ART

FOR THOUSANDS OF YEARS, artists have been inspired by the splendor of dawn and by flashing colors that streak across the sky as the sun sinks behind the sea. The intelligent force that drives the magnificence of the universe whispers its messages from eternity to anyone who sits still long enough to listen.

Several artists colonies and retreats are beautifully located for inspiring awe in the heart and mind of an artist. It is not surprising then that California, with her kaleidoscope of natural wonders, offers some of the best artists.

Dorland Mountain Arts Colony is a three hundred-acre nature preserve at the foothills of the Palomar Mountains, sixty miles north of San Diego. This artists colony provides each artist with simple living facilities for concentrated work within a setting of natural beauty.

Villa Montalvo in Saratoga specializes in visual arts and is located on 175 acres in the eastern foothills of the Santa Cruz mountains in a gorgeous Italian villa setting. Their mission statement: "We seek to provide artists from a wide range of backgrounds the benefits of a beautiful and inspiring location, where they are free to devote their time solely to creation and to the nourishment and engendering of the artistic process which provides a retreat from the pressures of work and family life, in which an eclectic community or artists from a multicultural base enrich each other."

Headland Center for the Arts in Marin County focuses on the visual arts. It is located on thirteen thousand coastal acres just across from the Golden Gate Bridge. Their mission statement is: "To foster creative investigations of the interdependence between human and natural systems."

LITERARY CALIFORNIA

AN OUTPOURING OF TALENT arrives in our state every day. Hopeful artists come to California in search of finding themselves, or losing themselves, or better yet being discovered, only to return home after a few tough years on the same bus on which they rolled in. Some stay longer. They've seen their friends, or more often, a friend of a friend, finally get that big break of which so many artists dream. From the overnight sensation to those struggling one baby step at a time, about the only thing that remains consistent is that there will always be something to write home about.

Our mythology began long ago. In 1510, Garcí Ordoñez de Montalvo wrote, "Know ye that on the right hand of the Indies there is an island called California." Illusion already under way. Our state's mystique is the prism though which the entire world watches, where the changing times keep adding to the colors that make California a writer's paradise.

Bret Harte was an important figure on California's literary scene, famous for his gold rush stories. In 1868, he cofounded *The Overland Monthly,* which cast a California spell on aspiring writers all across the country.

Samuel Clemens was on the run from an uproar that his articles had caused in Nevada and San Francisco. While waiting for things to cool off, he headed for an old mining camp where he heard a bizarre tale about a jumping frog. He wrote a story called "The Celebrated Jumping Frog of Calaveras County," but he used his pen name, Mark Twain, to maintain a low profile. Celebrity status was instantaneous.

The Call of the Wild. San Francisco-born Jack London dreamed of becoming a writer. In 1893, the seventeen-year-old sailor returned to Oakland after several action-packed months aboard a seal-hunting schooner. He devoured books from the Oakland Library. London dropped out of Berkeley and devoted himself to his writing career by pawning his belongings, and drove himself night and day to write. When he was twenty-seven, he wrote *The Call of the Wild,* which turned his dream into a reality. The action and adventure in his books, along with the struggle for survival and raw emotion, made London one of the most widely read authors in the country. His home near Santa Rosa is now a state historical park. The moral of the story? Write on!

Native of California, John Steinbeck, wrote about the paradox of our state so well that he won the 1962 Nobel Prize for lifetime achievement in literature. He was born in Salinas in 1902 and studied at Stanford. Steinbeck began receiving recognition after he wrote *Tortilla Flat,* a novel about a scruffy group of characters near Monterey. Next came *The Grapes of Wrath,* about a poor family who migrated to California from Oklahoma, for which he won a Pulitzer Prize in 1940. Other classics include *Cannery Row, East of Eden,* and *The Winter of Our Discontent.* Several of Steinbeck's stories have been made into movies.

Louis L'Amour, longtime resident of Los Angeles, wrote eighty-six works of Western fiction.

Some of the country's favorite detective stories have been written by Californians. San Francisco detective Dashiell Hammett wrote *The Maltese Falcon* (1930) and *The Thin Man* (1932). Raymond Chandler created detective Philip Marlowe. Some of the seedier edges of Los Angeles were used for Ross McDonald's private eye, Lew Archer, and his creepy backdrop. From novelist Joseph Wambaugh, graduate of Cal State Los Angeles, came all the tough cop adventure stories.

William Saroyan of Fresno refused the Pulitzer Prize for his 1939 play, *The Time of Your Life,* saying that it was "no more great or good" than any of his other works.

Ray Bradbury, longtime resident of Los Angeles, is a writer of science fiction and short stories. He has published some twenty-five works including *Farenheit 451,* which he started in his parent's garage in Venice, California. It sold over four and a half million copies.

Joan Didion, born in 1934, wrote the novel *Run River* about her native Sacramento Valley and uses California culture, locale, and people as themes in *Play It as It Lays* and *A Book of Common Prayer.*

The term "beatnik" was coined by San Francisco columnist Herb Caen in 1958. The beat generation was filled with California writers who were committed to changing and documenting the times. The earliest voices of the movement were San Francisco poets Allen Ginsberg and Lawrence Ferlinghetti, owner of City Lights bookstore.

Amy Tan, who wrote *The Joy Luck Club* in 1989, is a San Jose State alumna.

In 1982, novelist Alice Walker wrote *The Color Purple.* She received an Honorary Degree from California Institute of the Arts in 1995.

San Francisco State alum Anne Rice is the author of many best-selling novels, including *Interview with a Vampire* and *The Vampire Lestat.*

Let's hear it for readers! Gregory Peck holds a special event at the Mark Taper Auditorium where his friends read live from famous works of literature. The actors choose their own material. One of Peck's favorite readings was when Tim Curry read Dylan Thomas's *A Child's Christmas in Wales.* Why does he do it? To encourage people to get back to what's important. Reading books!

Looks Like A Movie Star

Since the movies came to California from New Jersey nearly a hundred years ago, talented and beautiful people have been following in search of their fifteen minutes of fame. Many stayed and raised gorgeous little actors and filmmakers of their own. All of these genetic blessings are one reason people say that everyone in California looks like a movie star. Another is that most movie stars do live here, making name dropping and star sighting a regular occurrence in certain parts of the state. Show biz, Hollywood, Tinsel Town, "the business"—all different names for the same industry that is classic California. The film industry is right here and so are the celebrities that support it, both of which add to the unique quality of the Golden State. Here are a few names of Californians, from the past and the present, of whom perhaps you have heard.

★　★　★

Marilyn Monroe, the ultimate Hollywood star, was born Norma Jean Baker in Los Angeles in 1926. While her professional life was a success and looked good from the outside, her personal life was tragic. Like so many who seek fame and fortune in Hollywood, Marilyn Monroe learned the hard way: neither fame nor fortune bring intrinsic happiness. She was born the illegitimate daughter of a mentally disturbed mother, Gladys Baker, and father, Edward Mortenson, who deserted them both. Norma Jean was deprived, neglected, and sexually abused. At nine years old, she was moved from orphanages and foster homes until at sixteen she dropped out of high school and entered into an arranged marriage. The first *Playboy Magazine* ever published featured a nude Marilyn Monroe centerfold, and both exploded in popularity. Twentieth Century Fox signed her to a $125 per week starlet's contract. Marilyn Monroe became a world famous symbol of Hollywood—glamour and sex. She starred in some thirty films, including *Some Like It Hot, How to Marry a Millionaire,* and *Asphalt Jungle.* Her early death at age thirty-six increased the public's fascination with her life. She is one of the most written about stars of the twentieth century.

John Wayne, born Marion Michael Morrison, became famous for his "man's man" roles in Western films which include *Stagecoach* and *Red River.* In 1969, he won an Academy Award for his performance in *True Grit.* He lived and raised his family in Newport Beach, where Orange County's airport, the John Wayne Airport, is found.

Elizabeth Taylor was born in England in 1931 but became a major star after becoming a resident of California. At age thirteen, she starred in *National Velvet.* As an adult, she starred in many films including *Cleopatra, Giant, Butterfield 8,* and *Who's Afraid of Virginia Woolf?* Her performances in the last two films won her Oscars for Best Actress. She is known for her life of glamour (she is Hollywood's longest-reigning glamour queen), wealth (the 69.42 carat Cartier diamond), marriages (a lot), and generosity. Her work for AIDS research earned her the Jean Hersholt Humanitarian Award. She is one tough cookie that keeps coming back. And don't call her Liz, she prefers Elizabeth.

Shirley Temple Black was born in Santa Monica in 1928. By the age of six, the prodigy was a famous and talented actress, singer, and dancer. Temple starred in *Little Miss Marker, Rebecca of Sunnybrook Farm, The Little Princess,* and many other movies in the '30s. Some of the scenes from the film *Heidi* were filmed at Lake Arrowhead (set to look like the Swiss Alps). In 1969, President Richard Nixon chose her to be U.S. representative to the General Assembly of the United Nations. President Gerald Ford appointed her U.S. ambassador to Ghana in 1974, the same year that she became the first woman to hold the position of U.S. Chief of Protocol. President George Bush appointed her ambassador to Czechoslovakia.

San Francisco-born Clint Eastwood is most noted for his portrayal of the strong, silent types of the West and as the police officer "Dirty Harry." Eastwood doesn't just play a tough guy, he is a tough guy. After his plane crashed into the ocean when he was a GI, he swam three miles in the Pacific Ocean to safety. He is a producer, director, and actor. Eastwood has acted in many films including *Play Misty for Me, The Bridges of Madison County,* and *Absolute Power.* Eastwood served as mayor of Carmel from 1986 to 1988, removing all doubt that acting and politics aren't related.

Robert Redford was born in Santa Monica. Redford's most noted role is that of the "Sundance Kid" in *Butch Cassidy and the Sundance Kid.* Other films include *The Way We Were, The Sting, Barefoot in the Park, Out of Africa, Three Days of the Condor,* and *Sneakers.* He won the Academy Award for Best Director in 1980 for *Ordinary People.* Redford became a sex symbol, admired and swooned over by millions, of which I am one.

Santa Ana-born Michele Pffeifer once worked at a local supermarket and, if you were lucky, she checked your groceries. She grew up into Miss Orange County, and then she took off to Hollywood, right around the corner but another world away. She hit the big time with her roles in *Scarface* and gave memorable performances in *The Fabulous Baker Boys, The Witches of Eastwick, Married to the Mob, Dangerous Minds,* and *Dangerous Liaisons.* This talented, California beauty is a megastar who brings in big box-office bucks. Those Orange County girls, you've got to love them!

Actor, producer, director, screenwriter Tom Hanks was born in Concord, California. He was painfully shy but covered it up by being class clown. In high school, and later at Cal State Sacramento, he became involved in drama productions. His many film hits included *Big, Sleepless in Seattle,* and *You've Got Mail.* The Academy awarded him back-to-back Oscars for Best Actor in *Philadelphia* and *Forrest Gump.* In 1999, he was nominated for Best Actor in *Saving Private Ryan.*

Here's a short list of movie stars and where they went to school:

USC: Michael Landon, Tom Selleck, Cybill Shepard, John Wayne. **California Institute of the Arts:** Ed Harris, David Hasselhoff, Paul Ruebens. **UCLA:** Beau Bridges, Carol Burnette, James Dean, Rob Reiner, Tim Robbins. **Berkeley:** Ted Danson, Jack Palance, Alicia Silverstone, Sigourney Weaver, Reese Witherspoon. **UC Santa Barbara:** Michael Douglas. **Cal State Sacramento:** Tom Hanks. **San Francisco State:** Annette Benning, Dana Carvey, Danny Glover. **Cal State Fullerton:** Kevin Costner. **Cal State Northridge:** Richard Dreyfuss, Teri Garr, Deborah Winger. **San Diego State:**

Raquel Welch. **Cal Poly Pomona:** Forest Whitaker. **Cal State Long Beach:** Steve Martin.

Another California beauty is working her way up the charts to super-stardom. Los Angeles-born Gweneth Paltrow dropped her art history classes at UC Santa Barbara to pursue an acting career. During the summer of 1991, while standing in line with her producer father Bruce Paltrow and his friend Steven Spielberg to see *Silence of the Lambs,* Spielberg offered her a part in his upcoming film, *Hook.* She accepted right then and there, and the biz has kept her busy acting in thirteen films over the last eight years. At the 1999 Academy Awards, Paltrow accepted the Oscar for Best Actress in a Dramatic Role for her performance in *Shakespeare in Love.* And with great style, I might add.

The biggest box office draw in the world and heart throb du jour is another native Californian. Leonardo DiCaprio was born in Los Angeles in 1974. His mother named him after a Leonardo da Vinci painting that she was admiring in the Uffizi just as she got an aggressive kick in the stomach from her unborn son. DiCaprio has kept kicking and fighting his way to the top by struggling in commercials and TV shows, including *Romper Room* when he was five. DiCaprio's performance in *What's Eating Gilbert Grape* earned him an Academy nomination. Other roles have been in the films *Romeo and Juliet, Marvin's Room,* and *The Man in the Iron Mask.* But it was *Titanic,* the highest grossing movie of all time, that launched this California face and career into super stardom.

Reagan's Biggest Role

LIKE MILLIONS HAD DONE before him, Ronald Reagan came to California seeking fame and fortune as an actor. He was handed the American dream when he took the oath of office and was sworn in as fortieth president of the United States.

Ronald Wilson Reagan was born in Illinois in 1911 and came to Hollywood during the spring of 1937. Why? To act. Jack Warner of Warner Brothers Studio signed Reagan to a $200 a week acting contract. Over the next twenty years, Reagan acted in more than fifty movies. In 1942, he joined the Army Air Corps and became a captain. After the war ended, he went back to Hollywood to continue his acting career. From 1947 to 1952, and again in 1959, he was president of the Screen Actors Guild. Reagan was hired by General Electric to talk to workers and improve relations between them and the management. He was against big government and started adding politics to his talks. People encouraged him to run for public office and put his political ideals to work. In the '60s Reagan became active in the California Republican Party. He made a televised speech in favor of Senator Barry Goldwater, which many people remembered, and in 1966 Reagan ran for governor of California. He won by almost a million votes and served two terms in office. In 1976, Ronald Reagan ran for president and lost to Gerald Ford, but he ran again in 1980 and won by more than eight million votes. Ronald Reagan was the oldest man ever to become present. He became the fortieth president of the United States shortly before he turned seventy. After his presidency, the Reagans returned to Bel Air, California, where they currently reside. Out past the Ventura County line, in Simi Valley, is the Ronald Reagan Presidential Library and Museum.

CINEMATIC WONDERS

THE UNLIMITED IMAGINATIONS of reel wizards and movie magicians spring to life on film as they learn inspiring and groundbreaking filmmaking techniques. Their contributions support art and industry, reaching worldwide, making California the unparalleled creative oasis and rich fantasy adventureland that it is.

Filmmaking is one of the state's multibillion dollar industries and the one for which we are most famous. Movies and California go together like Bogie and Bacall. Since the first talky, *The Jazz Singer,* progress in the movies has come a long way. Here is a look at a few bigtime filmmakers.

From actor, director, producer Rob Reiner, alumnus of UCLA, came *This Is Spinal Tap, Stand By Me, When Harry Met Sally, Misery, A Few Good Men,* and *The American President.*

The godfather of cinema, Francis Ford Coppola, was born in Detroit, raised in Queens, and was ten years old when he made his first 8mm film as a way to distract and amuse himself after coming down with polio. Years later, he enrolled in UCLA for graduate work. While attending UCLA, he worked as an assistant to Roger Corman on several films. In 1969, he established American Zoetrope, an independent film production company based in San Francisco. He won an Oscar for his screenplay *Patton.* In 1971,

The Godfather won Best Picture, Coppola won the Oscar for writing the screenplay with Mario Puzo, and he was nominated for Best Director. *The Godfather* became one of the highest-grossing movies ever made. *The Godfather, Part II* grossed even higher and won six Academy Awards. By the time he was thirty-six, Coppola had won six Oscars. In addition he wrote the screenplay for *The Great Gatsby* and has directed many films, including *One from the Heart, Peggy Sue Got Married, Rumble Fish, Bram Stoker's Dracula, The Rainmaker,* and *Apocalypse Now.* And just to top it all off, this godfather of cinema received the D. W. Griffith Award for lifetime achievement from the Directors Guild of America.

Tim Burton was born in 1958 in Burbank and attended California Institute of the Arts. His credits as a director include *Pee-Wee's Big Adventure, Beetlejuice,* and *Batman.* He wrote the screenplay, directed, and produced *Edward Scissorhands.*

Chicago-born USC graduate Robert Zemeckis has given us some great films. And he gave his alma mater a truly milestone gift in the fall of 1998. The Oscar-winning director donated $5 million to establish a digital production facility that will enable the School of Cinema-Television to assimilate digital technology throughout its curriculum. Together with fellow USC alumnus George Lucas and university trustee Steven Spielberg's donations, USC students will have a one-of-a-kind center to provide the important hands-on digital technology experience vital in today's industry. Zemeckis wrote and directed the *Back to the Future* trilogy, has produced some fifteen films, including *Contact* and *Death Becomes Her,* and has directed over fifteen films, including *Who Framed Roger Rabbit, Romancing the Stone,* and the Academy Award-winning *Forrest Gump.*

Thom Mount, alumnus of California Institute of the Arts, produced *Tequila Sunrise, Bull Durham,* and *Common Ground.*

From USC are director Ron Howard (*Willow, Ed TV, Cocoon,* and *Splash*) and writer/director John Singleton *(Boyz N The Hood).*

George Lucas was born in Modesto, a farm center in the San Joaquin Valley, where he helped his father run a stationery store. After attending Modesto Junior College, he was a social science major interested in art who couldn't get into art school. He chose USC because of the film program, because film was close enough to photography. He started out at USC studying animation. Because he arrived at school with no preconceived notions and no prior experience in film, what eventually emerged was a tendency toward visual, abstract, and nonstory films. He says that film editing is his greatest strength. Lucas wrote and directed *American Graffiti,* an homage to his teen years in central California. The film was made for $700,000 by Universal, bringing them $50 million in rentals and drawing five Oscar nominations. With *Star Wars,* a film that broke all box-office records, Lucas set new standards for special effects and epic imagination. He created the now-classic *Indiana Jones* adventures and directed *Labyrinth* and *Howard the Duck.* He wrote and executive produced *Empire Strikes Back* and *Return of the Jedi.* Lucas started the George Lucas Educational Foundation out of his commitment to education. He believes that learning starts with a student's passion. The foundation encourages American voters to support what they say is their number one priority: improving public education. He is the head of three Lucas companies all located in Marin County: Lucasfilm Ltd., LucasArts Entertainment Company, and Lucas Digital Ltd. He recently pledged $1.5 million with his pal Robert Zemeckis to help build the new state-of-the-art digital facility at USC. He has won sixteen Oscars and received forty nominations. Lucas says everything he first learned about film, he learned at USC.

Steven Spielberg earned his BA in English and studied at Cal State Long Beach. His dream of directing began at age twelve. Spielberg created his first disaster scene with toy trains and plastic action figures and filmed it with the camera his father had received as a Father's Day gift. He staged another, rather larger, train disaster in his film *Close Encounters of the Third Kind.* Spielberg claims to have had some trouble when he was in school—sometimes with his studies, more often with the football players. When he was thirteen, he put an end to the trouble by asking one of them to star in the war movie he was making that weekend. Spielberg liked to edit his weekend work on Mondays. Just like Elliot did in *E.T.,* a trick that kept Spielberg out of school was holding the thermometer next to a light bulb, which causes the mercury to rise quickly. Obviously, his mother was not in the room at the time. Spielberg spent some time during the summer of 1965 with his cousin in Canoga Park, close to Universal Studios, and after showing executives some of his 8mm work, he was advised to shoot something in 16- or 35mm. The boy wonder presented his 24-minute short *Amblin* at the Atlantic Film Festival, and it earned the twenty year old a seven-year contract with Universal-MCA. Later he went on to create his own independent company, Amblin Entertainment. He is a writer, executive producer, and director. He has produced and directed many fine films, including *Saving Private Ryan, Men in Black, Amistad, Jurassic Park, Schindler's List, Gremlins, The Color Purple, Raiders of the Lost Ark, Close Encounters of the Third Kind,* and *Jaws.*

Insiders tip: The mechanical shark in *Jaws* was named Bruce, after Spielberg's lawyer. Steven Spielberg, sometimes referred to in the biz as "Spielrock," has been catapulted into mogul standing and has won many awards, including Academy Awards and the American Film Institute Life Achievement Award. He has produced a string of A-list movies, generated billions of dollars in the industry, and given back millions to his community. In addition, he is married to Cate Capshaw and has seven children! Spielberg recently signed on with $500,000 to help his pal George Lucas build a new digital facility at USC. This is a very busy guy. And generous too.

RANDOM FILM STUFF

THE ACADEMY OF MOTION PICTURE ARTS AND SCIENCES was organized in Los Angeles in May 1927. Douglas Fairbanks Sr., the Academy's founding president, gave the first lecture at USC, and in doing so, initiated America's first film program. Among the Academy's purposes are encouraging educational activity between the public and the professional community, advancing the arts and sciences of motion pictures, and fostering cooperation among cultural leaders for creative, technical, and educational progress. Many of its six thousand members are California residents. The first awards ceremony took place in the Blossom Room at the Hollywood Roosevelt Hotel. Tickets cost $10, attendance was 250, and 15 statuettes were awarded. Today the Academy Awards is a live, worldwide telecast. On only three occasions has the presentation been interrupted: in 1938, when destructive floods nearly washed out Los Angeles; in 1968, as a gesture of respect for Dr. Martin Luther King, who had been assassinated; and 1981, due to the assassination attempt on President Ronald Reagan. In all three cases, the show was aired after postponements and delays. After all, the show must go on!

California's first theater, the Eagle, was built on the Embarcadero in Sacramento. A replica of the Eagle stands today in Old Sacramento.

And the winner is—*Gone With the Wind* released in 1939, which generated more income than any other pre–World War II movie. If the income of the film could be adjusted to allow for inflation, it could be regarded as the most successful movie ever made since the period of its release. It won eight Academy Awards out of thirteen nominations.

Emerging African-American filmmakers can showcase their work at USC, the site for the annual Hollywood Black Film Festival. The event is held in February.

How much would you pay to own an Oscar? From Christie's in Los Angeles, Clark Gable's Oscar *for It Happened One Night* sold for $607,500 on December 15, 1993.

Same night, same place, same actor, same movie: Clark's personal script fetched $244,500. Perhaps it was gold-leafed.

Zuma Beach, near Malibu, was the setting for *Beach Blanket Bingo* and *Dead Man's Curve.*

It is rumored that Hotel Del Coronado near San Diego provided L. Frank Baum with the the inspiration for the Emerald City when he wrote *The Wizard of Oz.*

Big-time Hollywood jobs held by university alumni:

USC:

Laura Ziskin, President, Fox 2000 Twentieth Century Fox, Inc.

Michelle Manning, President of Production, Paramount Pictures. Brian Grazer, CEO Imagine Entertainment.

Scott Sassa, President, NBC Entertainment, past President, Turner Entertainment Group.

UCLA:

Mike Medavoy, former Chairman, Tri-Star Pictures, cofounder Orion Pictures.

UC Santa Cruz:

Lindsay Loray, President, United Arts Pictures and producer of the Oscar-winning film *Sense and Sensibility.*

Producer of *Batman* and *Rainman,* Peter Guber, has taught at UCLA for over twenty-five years and cochairs their Producers Program.

Longtime California resident Hugh Hefner donated $1.5 million for the study of American film to USC.

Painting California

California's mythology has been casting its spell on resident and visiting artists for a very long time. The ever-changing environment, the gentle breezes, and the sea glorify the state as a land of beauty in which to paint. Throughout its history, California has been depicted by artists. Both our state's history and the expression of the artist's spirit is reflected though California art.

★   ★   ★

The oldest known watercolor sketch of California in this country is *View of Monterey* by John Sykes, done between the years 1790 and 1795. It can be seen at the Oakland Museum of California. During the age of exploration, a necessary part of the crew was often a professional artist, who had the task of depicting the topography of the country being explored. Sykes was the artist for the Pacific Expedition voyage. Sykes was born in 1773 and was seventeen when he embarked upon this, his first journey. The Admiralty in London possesses most of John Sykes's works.

The first known view of San Francisco is titled *View of the Spanish Establishments of San Francisco in New California* by Georg Heinrich Von Langsdorff, done in 1806. This ink-on-paper sketch depicts a cluster of adobe buildings, behind which lies a gentle rise of open land, with Indians paddling their canoe in the foreground. *Dance of the Indians at Mission San Jose* portrays six Indians in body paint with feather costumes and ornaments. The highlights of

Langsdorff's trip were a series of Indian dances in his honor and the sight of a California bear. Both paintings are at the Oakland Museum of California.

Ernest Etienne Narjot de Francheville was a forty-niner and was one of the first artists attracted to the West by news of gold. He spent his first years as a miner and then went to work in San Francisco in the field of art. Francheville became widely known for character sketches, portraits, and murals, many of which were destroyed in the earthquake and fire of 1906. His last great commission was to paint murals in Leland Stanford's Palo Alto tomb, but after paint got in his eyes from painting the ceiling, he suffered complete blindness. Francheville died in 1898 in San Francisco. Both *Placer Operations at Foster's Bar* and *Days of Gold* are part of the Honeyman Collection at the Oakland Museum of California.

One of the most famous paintings of the gold rush is called *Sunday Morning in the Mines* by Charles Christian Nahl. It is in the Crocker Art Museum in Sacramento.

Maurice Braun of Hungary settled in San Diego in 1910. His light-filled landscapes expressed theosophical principles, and he became San Diego's first nationally recognized artist. *California Valley Farm,* his oil on canvas, is part of the Collection of Joseph L. Moure Frontispiece.

Arthur F. Mathews, raised in Oakland, inspired a generation of Northern California artists and was known for the decorative aesthetic movement and tonalist landscapes.

With his oil paintings and ceramics, turn-of-the-twentieth-century artist, Franz Bischoff, helped make the rose a symbol of Pasadena.

Guy Rose was the first native of Southern California to receive international fame. After living in Giverny, France, he returned to Pasadena in 1914. He was a California Impressionist who painted both coastal and inland scenes of Carmel and Laguna Beach.

The Society of Six was an association formed in Oakland in 1917. It was made up of six painters who were, at the time, considered "rough." Their goal was to paint the local landscape of the Bay Area through their own energetic expression, which included shockingly vivid colors and bold brushwork. They were Selden Gile, Maurice Logan, William Clapp, August Gay, Bernard von Eichman, and Louis Siegreist. Today they are today recognized as the pioneers of modernism in Northern California.

Leading American Impressionist, Childe Hassam, first came to San Francisco for the Panama-Pacific International Exposition in 1915. The Exposition had commissioned a piece of artwork. Hassam made several painting excursions to Carmel and into Southern California.

Major California plein-air painter, Granville Redmond, was raised in San Jose and trained in Paris. He painted impressionist landscapes from Laguna Beach to Tiberon and is best known for his images of poppy fields.

Lee Blair is a California-born watercolorist who created bustling genre scenes of Los Angeles. He is a leader in the animation and film industry and lives near Santa Cruz. His watercolor on paper done in 1938, *San Francisco Cable Car Celebration,* is part of the Sally and David Martin Collection.

David Hockney, the English-born artist, came to Los Angeles in 1964. His first California images, for which he is most famous, are of swimming pools. *A Bigger Splash,* acrylic on canvas (1967), is at the Tate Gallery, London. *Mulholland Drive: The Road to the Studio,* acrylic on two canvases, is at the Los Angeles County Museum of Art.

Richard Diebenkorn was a leading California contemporary modernist first known as a San Francisco Bay Area expressionist. He taught at UCLA between 1966 and 1973. He is now identified with abstract interpretations of California's light and open space.

Native of Omaha, Edward Ruscha, moved to California in 1956 and has become one of Los Angeles's most famous contemporary artists. His pop art and images of billboard signs, gas stations, and Los Angeles are transformed into idealized symbols.

Wayne Thiebaud is a pop interpreter of the urban streets and highways of California. In 1966, he began depicting rural Sacramento.

Betye Saar was born in 1926 and grew up in Pasadena. In the '40s she attended Pasadena City College, and in 1949 she graduated from UCLA. Her art form grew into painting images of spirit and magic and placing treasures in the medium of boxes. After being deeply angered at the death of Reverend Martin Luther King Jr., she used her boxes to make strong political statements, one of which she named *The Liberation of Aunt Jemima*. Saar began to gain recognition within the larger art world, winning great honors and awards. In 1987, she began including computer circuit boards in her work. After her magic touch, the metallic circles and wires become a night filled with stars and constellations. Saar's art unites the spirit of all races and people.

Some of the world's most famous art can be found in several world-famous California museums: The Crocker Art Museum in Sacramento, J. Paul Getty Museum in Los Angeles, Los Angeles County Museum of Art, the San Francisco Museum of Modern Art, Norton Simon Museum in Pasadena, and the California Palace of the Legion of Honor in San Francisco.

EXPRESSIONS OF ART

A SIXTY-SEVEN YEAR DESERT DWELLER named Leonard Knight has spent the last fourteen years painting a hillside at the end of a road eighty miles southeast of Palm Springs. He has turned the bluff into his own unique wall of art, a multicolored hill that he calls Salvation Mountain. On the side he painted: God Is Love. It seems that the artistic spirit has always moved Californians to create.

★   ★   ★

Every self-respecting California town has had a theater since the gold rush days. The theatrical arts flourished after statehood and continue to flourish today. California has also influenced contemporary drama. With its over-the-top parodies, San Francisco's long-running *Beach Blanket Babylon* entertains visitors and locals alike.

The San Francisco Mime Troupe combines radical politics and commedia dell'arte forms.

Susanville in Lassen County proudly depicts its history in huge murals located on buildings throughout the Historic Uptown District.

Simon Rodia was an Italian immigrant who settled in California in the 1920s. He purchased a triangular lot of land at 1765 East 107th Street in South Central Los Angeles. There he created the one hundred foot-tall towers now known as the Watts Towers. The steel is decorated with a mosaic of materials Rodia collected during the thirty-three years it took him to build the towers. The Watts Towers are now a state historic park.

Los Angeles is the western home of the Joffrey Ballet.

The plein air style of painting distinguished the art colony of Laguna Beach in the 1920s.

Musician Jerry Garcia, artist Gary Wyland, and Joe Boxer (as in the underwear) custom-designed guest rooms at the Hotel Triton in San Francisco.

Walt Disney founded the California Institute of the Arts in Valencia where imagination runs wild.

Isaac Stern was born in Russia and emigrated to San Francisco at age one. When he was eleven, he made an impressive debut with the San Francisco Symphony. He has recorded and played with major international orchestras around the world and helped the careers of many important musicians.

Martha Graham grew up in Santa Barbara. She became one of the most influential modern dancers of the twentieth century.

Which library contains a Gutenberg Bible and one of the finest rare-book collections of Shakespeare? The Huntington near Pasadena.

The world's highest-funded art collections are at the **Getty Museum** in Los Angeles.

More than two hundred outdoor murals can be found in the Mission District of San Francisco. On Stockton Street in Chinatown, the Chinatown mural is a half-block long.

Ansel Adams, born in San Francisco, was one of the nation's foremost photographic artists. He first visited Yosemite in 1916. Adams became most noted for his dynamic black-and-white photos of Yosemite and other Western wilderness areas. Another of his trademarks are sharply focused, finely detailed photographs of small objects in nature. Adams helped found the department of photography at the San Francisco Art Institute.

Los Angeles has both a Museum of Neon Art and a Sci-fi Monster Museum.

Mark Twain wrote of his California experiences in *Roughing It* in 1852.

There are eighty thousand panes of stained glass in the domed ceiling of the Sheraton Palace Hotel in San Francisco.

A Free-Spirit

ISADORA DUNCAN was born on May 26, 1877 in San Francisco. While her mother worked, Isadora was left alone and spent much of her time walking by the sea, creating dreams and fantasies of her own. Music, poems, and the sea inspired her to move her body to the rhythm of their worldly beat. Her movements reflected what she felt inside. At six years old, Isadora announced to her mother that she was a dancer and a revolutionary. She began teaching neighborhood children in their backyard, which they turned into an amateur theater. Isadora became involved in San Francisco theater when, at the turn of the century, it was at its height. She was unconventional and claimed the human body as a temple, the solar plexus as the center of all energy. She was inclined to speak of the soul and the spirit, and write symbolically about mythology, nature, and love. She began her dancing career in San Francisco and eventually traveled around the world teaching. She influenced and inspired much of what exists today as modern dance.

The San Francisco Ballet

ORIGINALLY THE SAN FRANCISCO BALLET was an auxiliary to the San Francisco Opera, which opened in 1851, making it the oldest existing ballet company in America. Today the ballet operates as an independent organization, founded by Adolph Bolm in 1933, and has become highly regarded artistically. In describing the San Francisco Ballet, it is common to hear words like beautifully trained, buoyantly elegant, and attractive stylistic openness. The San Francisco Ballet is world class.

The company's eclectic choreographic works have been widely applauded, ranging from full-length revivals of *Swan Lake* and the *Nutcracker* to twentieth century classics by Ashton, Balanchine, and other leading choreographers and newer works by its own composers. This company doesn't believe in relying on a "star system," rather, it builds a true ensemble company with marked success. Bravo!

A MUSICAL NOTE

Traditional songs as part of Indian ceremonial and religious experience are used to help express feelings or to focus the mind. Sometimes a song belongs to one particular person. Many Indians feel that, just as an animal might come to a certain person, so too comes a song. When this is the case, the song is thought of as a living thing that allows itself to be sung only by the person to whom it revealed itself. Drums and gourd rattles are made and used as instruments, but Indian music, characterized by syllabic melodies, is primarily vocal.

In old California, Spanish and Mexican folk songs were born of emotion. The music held a particular naïveté yet vividness of life that was both willful and rich in melody. Back then everybody sang; folk songs accompanied cowpunchers who rode along just as they accompanied women waiting back home on the range. This Latin-based music flowered in the California of old and continues to be renewed in California today.

Franciscan missionaries, who settled throughout the state between 1769 and 1834, introduced music based on seventeenth and eighteenth century Spanish and Mexican church music. Choirs and bands that used Western instruments such as flutes, violins, and trumpets were organized. The music is now known as "California mission music." The most prominent missionary music educator was Spanish composer Marciso Duran, who compiled the *Mission San Jose Choir Book*.

The forty-niners brought with them both raucous ballads and a bit of high culture. When San Francisco became a boomtown in 1848, frontier conditions rapidly created an active musical life. The largely male population craved opportunities to hear music of their own culture, especially the Italian and German immigrants. Traveling musicians hosted concerts in remote mining towns, and soon regular performances were given in San Francisco.

The first internationally known pianist to perform in San Francisco was Henri Herz. At his debut, he was paid a pan of gold dust worth $10,000. Since then music in California has grown into a rich and diverse offering of creativity and passion. One out of every eight music festivals and concerts in the nation is held in California.

The San Francisco Art Association was formed in 1871 by a group of creative souls who shared a common love of art. Just after the raucous period of the gold rush, they helped define the heart of the cultural community in San Francisco. Its future would grow out of the state's most abundant resource: creativity. San Francisco today offers more cultural attractions per capita than any other American city.

The parents of Yehudi Menuhin were descendants of Palestine Jews, poor, recently married, and postgraduate students at New York University. In 1916, they gave birth to Yehudi and one year later moved to San Francisco. When Yehudi was four, he begged for a violin. His formal debut came in 1924 in conjunction with the San

Francisco Symphony Orchestra when he was seven years old. He played de Bériot's "Scène de Ballet" at Oakland Auditorium. One year later, Yehudi was a soloist with the San Francisco Symphony. Within the next year or so, he made debuts in New York and Europe. By age sixteen, Yehudi was a full-fledged professional artist devoting half the year to appearances in Europe and America, filling audiences with musical celebrities and leaders of society. Considered a prodigy of prodigies, Yehudi Menuhin became one of the greatest box office attractions the concert world had ever known.

The Central Avenue-based Los Angeles jazz scene, with particular focus on the years 1917–29, was hot and contributed greatly to the history of American jazz. The first recordings ever made by an African-American jazz band, a group led by **Edward "Kid" Ory,** were recorded in Los Angeles. **The Creole Band,** which played a major role in disseminating New Orleans-style jazz, was actually formed in Los Angeles, the same city where Jelly Roll Morton's first compositions were published. Before achieving fame in Duke Ellington's orchestra, trombonists **Britt Woodman** and **Lawrence Brown** had first professionally established themselves in, you guessed it, Los Angeles.

Jazz musician Stan Kenton, who initiated several progressive-jazz ensembles throughout the country, gained early fame at Balboa Pavilion in Orange County.

When the movies started to include sound and became talkies in 1927, Hollywood needed composers and performers like crazy. Film scores were composed, and the studios employed orchestras of symphonic proportions. A vast pool of musical talent developed in Los Angeles, the center of the recording industry.

David Raskin came to Hollywood in 1935 to arrange Charlie Chaplain's music for *Modern Times* and went on to write and score music for over a hundred films. An Academy Award-winning film composer who has taught at UCLA for over twenty years, Raskin is best known for composing the theme song for 1944's *Laura*. This guy lived the golden glam days of Hollywood and has plenty of great dish!

During World War II, Southern African Americans came to work in the shipyards and brought with them a style of dancing that came to be known as West Coast Swing. California-based artists like **Chet Baker** and native **Dave Brubeck** helped develop the sound by combining small groups, complex harmonies, and improvisation.

California has twelve major opera companies, ten major symphony orchestras, and fourteen major dance companies. The Los Angeles Philharmonic and the San Francisco Symphony orchestras are among the world's prestigious symphonic ensembles. San Diego and San Francisco each have a world-class resident opera company. Oakland and San Francisco both have a resident ballet company. In addition, California has 18 classical choral groups, 216 dance groups, and 37 other symphony orchestras. Heaven!

The San Fransisco Opera

Bᴇʟʟɪɴɪ's *LA SONNAMBULA*, the first opera heard in San Francisco, was performed on January 24, 1852, by the touring Pellegrini Opera troupe. In 1869, when railroads joined the east and west coasts, San Francisco took on the socioeconomic character of eastern cities and opera expanded rapidly. Nearly five thousand operatic performances were given between 1852 and the great earthquake of 1906.

San Fransisco's most beloved diva at the turn of the century was Luisa Tetrazzini, who performed at the Tivoli Opera House. On Christmas Eve, 1910, she lent a legendary operatic moment to the city when she stood on a platform at the corner of 3rd and Kearny and sang arias to the delighted crowd in the streets.

In 1922, Gaetano Merola started the San Francisco Opera. San Francisco was the first American city to have an opera house that was not built by and for a small group of rich patrons. Its first season was in Exposition Auditorium, which is now the Bill Graham Civic Auditorium in the Civic Center. The barn-like structure seated six thousand. War Memorial Opera House opened in 1932. Some opera heroes and heroines that performed there were Luciano Pavarotti, Jess Thomas, Lawrence Tibbett, Thomas Steward, Georgio Tozzi, Richard Lewis, Licia Albanese, Ezio Pinza, James McCracken, Jose Carreras, Kirsten Flagstad, Bianca Saroya, Lily Pons, Lotte Lehmann, Claudia Muzio, Joan Sutherland, Frederica von Stade, Regina Resnik, and Tatiana Troyanos.

In 1969, Pavarotti was in the middle of performing the second act of *La Bohème* when the chandeliers began to shake and the building to rumble. "What the hell is going on," he hissed to the prompter. But calm was restored as Pavarotti continued to sing and never missied a beat. *Bellisima!*

Balboa Park

WHAT PARK IS ONE THIRD LARGER than New York's Central Park? Yes, Balboa Park in San Diego. This 1,200-acre urban park is home to over eighty-five organizations: fifteen museums, various performing arts, international culture associations, as well as the San Diego Zoo. All this fabulousness make it the largest cultural complex west of the Mississippi.

The world-famous Old Globe Theater in Balboa Park is San Diego's largest arts organization. On its three stages, the Old Globe annually presents at least twelve productions and 550 performances. Stage productions range from Shakespeare to Neil Simon. In 1984 the Old Globe Theater received American theater's highest accolade: the special Antoinette Perry (Tony) Award for excellence. The theater has certainly had its share of impressive guests! Topping the list is Her Majesty Queen Elizabeth II who visited in 1983. In 1989 Thorton Wilder's *The Skin of Our Teeth* was telecast live.

The rich ethnic diversity of California is reflected in the Park's institutions. Among them are the Centro Cultural de la Raza, the WorldBeat Center celebrating cultures of African origins, the Japanese Friendship Gardens, and the House of Pacific Relations consisting of seventeen cottages—home to thirty groups of diverse national origins. A walk in Balboa park is hard to beat.

The San Francisco Symphony

THE SAN FRANCISCO SYMPHONY gave its first concert in 1911 and in 1926 it was the first symphony to be heard on the radio. Today it is world renowned. Among the awards it has won are Japan's Record Academy Award, France's Grand Prix du Disque, Britain's Gramaphone Award, America's Grammy Award for Carmina Burana, Brahms, Berman Requiem, and scenes from Prokofiev's *Romeo and Juliet*.

Since 1986 the Symphony has made three tours of Asia, five of Europe, including their debut at the Salzburg Festival, and has traveled extensively throughout the U.S. Some important conductors who have guest conducted are Bruno Walster, Leopold Stokowski, Leonard Bernstein, Sir George Solti, and Kurt Masur. Important composers who have led the orchestra include Stravinsky, Prokofiev, Ravel, Schoenberg, and Copland.

Past directors have been Henry Hadey, Alfred Hertz, Basil Cameron, Issay Dobrowen, Pierre Monteux, Enrique Jorda, Josef Krips, Seiji Ozawa, Edo de Waart, and Herbert Blomstedt. The symphony today is directed by Michael Tilson Thomas.

The Hollywood Bowl

UNDER THE STARS at the Hollywood Bowl on July 11, 1922, conductor Alfred Herz and the Los Angeles Philharmonic inaugurated the °rst season of music for an audience seated on simple wooden benches. Situated in the natural setting of the Hollywood hills, the Bowl today is one of the largest natural amphitheaters in the world with a seating capacity of 18,000.

In 1928, Myron Hunt, who designed the Rose Bowl in Pasadena, designed the balloon shaped seating area that embraces the surrounding hillside. In 1928, Frank Lloyd Wright's oldest son, Frank Wright, designed the music shell which inspired the current shell which was built in 1980 by internationally-renowned Los Angeles architect, Frank Gehry.

The Bowl has been the summer home to the Los Angeles Philharmonic since 1922 and to the Hollywood Bowl Orchestra since 1991. In the 1930s Stokowski led the Philharmonic. Other legendary conductors who have led include Itzhak Perlman, Vladimir Horowitz, Plácido Domingo, Beverly Sills, and Isaac Stern. Legendary artists who have appeared at the bowl include Sinatra, Pavirotti, Streisand, Stravinsky, and Heifetz. Fred Astaire, Fonteyn and Nureyev, the Bolshoi Ballet, and Baryshnikov have danced there. Billie Holiday, Nat "King" Cole, Ella Fitzgerald, Al Jolson, and Judy Garland have headlined as have the Beatles, The Doors, Elton John, and Garth Brooks. The all-time highest attendance record, however, was 26,410, set on August 11, 1936, for the French opera star, Lily Pons.

The Hollywood Bowl has been a success since its first season and remains a symbol of California glamour and romance. Whatever your choice of entertainment, whether classical or rock and roll, an evening under the stars at the Hollywood Bowl is sure to be a hit.

MORRISON

I'd won a bet on an east/west high school game and the wager was that the loser had to buy tickets to the 1969 Fourth of July Doors concert at the Hollywood Bowl. The opening act was the Chambers Brothers followed by Steppenwolf. And then the Doors came on. I remember from out of the dark thousands of sparklers firing off during "Light My Fire." But the best moment, to me, was during the song "The Unknown Soldier," when the gunshot went off and Jim Morrison appeared to lay dead on the stage.

COLONEL PEN, Barstow

Rockin' & Rollin'

THE SOUND OF CALIFORNIA rock and roll has deluged the recording business for five decades and has been largely instrumental in its development. Local artists, as well as hopeful musicians, come from far and wide, bringing with them an enormous range of musical influence. And as always, the times through which each generation lives is reflected through the music.

The fun-loving doo-wop bands of the '50s changed into the freaky free-love San Francisco sound of the '60s. With flowers in their hair, people everywhere were dancing in the street, while a turn of the radio dial took us further south where beach blanket teen idols were catching a wave and California girls. Singer-songwriters and California-flavored country-western music kept people rockin' through the life in the fast-lane '70s. When metal exploded onto the L.A. scene in the '80s, once again the Sunset Strip came alive; tattoos and torn T-shirts, Harleys and big hair, the guitar was the heavy and metal became a lifestyle choice. Like a shot in the night, the one-time quiet storm that voiced urban concerns through rhythm and blues has turned into rap and soul, the most significant musical development in the '90s.

The times keep changing and with it the music. Much musical influence and lifestyle choice starts right here in California—always a beat ahead.

★   ★   ★

In the '50s, doo-wop was hot. The singers who didn't sing lead got tired of only singing "aaaaah," so for variety they made up two nonsense syllables. One of the biggest of the doo-wop bands was from the West Coast, hence their name, **The Coasters**. With songs like "Charlie Brown," "Yakety Yak," and "Along Came Jones," The Coasters were one of only two doo-wop bands that survived into the '60s.

The most requested doo-wop song of all time is "Earth Angel" by a garage band that started out of a South Los Angeles residential neighborhood. **The Penguins,** who named themselves after the Kool cigarette trademark, were all students at Fremont High School in Los Angeles.

What do you get when the West Coast music, movie, and television industries merge? West Coast teen idols! One time Mouseketeer turned beach blanket babe, **Annette Funicello,** had eight big hits on Walt Disney's Vista label.

Connie Stevens, Roger Smith, and **Ed "Kookie" Burns,** from the television shows *Hawaiian Eye* and *77 Sunset Strip*, were signed by the new label that Warner Brothers started. Gidget, as well as girls all over the country, swooned over **James Darren,** the singing star of *Gidget* movie fame. *The Donna Reed Show* gave us **Shelley Fabares,** who gave us "Johnny Angel." Other singing teen idol stars were **Bobby Vee, Connie Francis,** and **Brenda Lee.** Perhaps one of the most successful and talented singing star from that fun-loving era was **Ricky Nelson,** who made his start on *The Adventures of Ozzie and Harriet*. His rockabilly-pop band was one of the best and is most remembered for the teen ballads "Dreamin" and "You're Sixteen."

In the early '60s a large contingent of local instrumental bands developed when **Dick Dale-style music** was all the rage. Big hits like "Wipeout," "Pipeline," and "Let's Go Trippin'" celebrated California living through a wave of instrumental sound.

Mike Love plus Al Jardine plus Carl Dennis and Brian Wilson equal the **Beach Boys.** These California boys turned California's sound of surf music into an overnight, countrywide sensation. Brian Wilson emerged as the band's leader, but not as your typical rock star. Wilson, a musical genius, played his falsetto and used unorthodox harmony structures for rock. His masterful arrangements and lyrics that sang out of "Fun Fun Fun" and "Surfin' USA" sent out such "Good Vibrations" that California became the one state in the country in which everyone wanted to be.

Rock and roll started changing its tune with the California folk sound of the '60s. **The Byrds,** with David Crosby, wrote the first rock and roll album with a message: "Mr. Tambourine Man." "Turn Turn Turn" became The Byrds's second number one hit.

The San Francisco sound developed around the little-known area of Haight and Ashbury and the campuses and outskirts of Berkeley and Stanford. Bohemian bands in the forefront were **The Charlatans, Big Brother and the Holding Company, The Grateful Dead, Jefferson Airplane,** and **Buffalo Springfield.**

Folk singer **Joe McDonald of Country Joe and the Fish,** as well as **Moby Grape, Sonny and Cher,** and the **Mamas and the Papas** all contributed to the freaky free-love scene. The Haight passed the acid test; its heyday was 1967.

Some of the first rock and roll records in the Bay Area were from a streetfighter raised on the wrong side of San Francisco Bay. After a music theory course in high school, Sylvester Stewart of **Sly and the Family Stone** was at the turning point of the pop scene. Sly preached the ghetto's message of hope with the song "Everyday People," while "I Want to Take You Higher" expressed the sentiments of the Haight. In 1971, the album *There's a Riot Going On*, with the hit single "Family Affair," was perfectly timed. Sly and the Family Stone's music is unforgettable. Their black testimony of the early '70s was some of the first, and its effect has been everlasting.

They had been together since high school, but they couldn't decide on a name. From El Cerrito, a suburb near Oakland, **Creedence Clearwater Revival** started out as the Blue Velvets and then changed to the Golliwogs. In 1969 and 1970, Creedence was the most popular rock and roll band in the nation. "Proud Mary" was their first big hit, followed up with political songs like "Fortunate Son" and "Don't Look Now." **John** and **Tom Fogerty, Doug Clifford,** and **Stu Cook** expressed the emotional and turbulent times of the day through several top ten songs like "Who'll Stop the Rain," "Green River," "Heard It through the Grapevine," and "Bad Moon Rising."

As the days grew darker in the early '70s so did the music. **Jim Morrison** was a poet and film student at UCLA who drifted out to the transient culture of Venice Beach. Morrison, on the beach one day, ran into fellow student and keyboard player, **Ray Manzarek.** Morrison and Manzarek conceptualized **The Doors** that day as they sat cross-legged in the sand and Morrison sang his lyrics. The Doors started out at the dingy clubs along the Sunset Strip. Morrison's morbid obsessions about death and dread got the band thrown out of The Whiskey after singing "The End," which was only their first of many similar historical claims. The album *The Doors* with the single, "Light My Fire," became one of the best-selling albums of the era. After completing the album *LA Woman,* Morrison left Los Angeles and flew to Paris. The lost angel was twenty-seven years old when he died of a heart attack on July 3, 1971.

On the flip side of the dark sound was the wholesomeness of the **Carpenters,** the **Osmonds,** and **Shaun Cassidy.** Great L.A. soul came from **Earth, Wind & Fire.**

Linda Ronstadt emerged as a Los Angeles rock star in 1975 with her hit "You're No Good." Rondstadt's long-standing success is due in large part to her voice, one of the strongest, most alluring, and most versatile in pop music.

The Eagles epitomized Los Angeles in the '70s with their song "Life in the Fast Line" from the album *Hotel California.* They became the most commercial American rock group of the '70s.

When California natives Stevie Nicks and Lindsay Buckingham joined forces with Britishers Christine McVie and Mick Fleetwood, **Fleetwood Mac** was born. The group developed the quintessential California sound on the albums *Fleetwood Mac* and *Rumors.* This band probably sold more records than any of the Southern California bands.

The Knack was one of the first California punk bands to emerge. Fans slam-danced to **Black Flag,** the **Germs,** the **Circle Jerks** and, one of the best, **X**. The Whiskey a Go Go learned to put away tables and chairs as the dance floor become a mosh pit.

The '80s also brought the reemergence of girl bands. California girls have often been sung about, but the **Bangles** and the **Go-Gos** put a new twist on things by doing the singing themselves. The five Southern California party girls that made up the Go-Gos became so popular they won a place in history by becoming the first all-girl band to make a number one album.

Headbangers in the '80s brought the Sunset Strip alive like it hadn't been since The Doors knocked it dead. **Motley Crüe, Van Halen, Ratt, Quiet Riot, Guns 'n Roses, Metallica,** and **Bad Religion** are all California bands. The Guns n' Roses album *Appetite for Destruction* is considered one of the best rock and roll albums ever made.

California native **Bonnie Raitt** aspired to be the female Muddy Waters. Eighteen years into her career, she began receiving recognition. Raitt is a master slide guitarist and the first woman to have a guitar named after her. She swept the 1989 Grammy Awards and is today one of the most admired musicians in the business.

Pop and rock singer **Natalie Cole,** a California native, had a string of lead R&B singles between 1975 and 1978. In the '90s she returned to her roots and recorded some of her father, Nat King Cole's, classic songs. In a tribute to him, she recorded the album *Unforgettable With Love*. It sold eight million copies in 1991 and competed with Metallica for the number-one spot on the charts for several weeks. *Unforgettable With Love* was nominated for seven Grammy awards in 1992 including song, album, and record of the year. Natalie Cole went home with seven Grammy awards that night. This is one class-act that keeps coming back.

The most significant musical development in to the '90s was rap. **Dr. Dre, Snoop Doggy Dogg, Cypress Hill,** and **Ice's T** and **Cube** put West Coast rap on the charts. Dr. Dre is considered the most influential rapper/producer of his time. His straight-out-of-Compton attitude has created his own style of hip-hop. He coined the term and sound commonly known as gangsta-rap.

Snoop Doggy Dogg grew up in Long Beach and a life of crime and was in and out of prison. His best friend was **Warren G,** Dr. Dre's brother. Snoop's dream of pursuing music came true when Dre arranged to have Snoop sing his rhymes on Dr. Dre's album *The Chronic* and the single "Ain't Nuthin' but a G-Thang." Snoop's first album, *Doggystyle,* was the first debut album ever to enter the charts at number one.

In 1995, **Tupak Shakur's** album *Me Against the World* established Shakur as one of the most popular rappers of the '90s. He signed with Death Row Records, and in 1996 his album *All Eyez on Me* sold six million records. On September 13, 1996, on his way to a charity event, tragically Shakur was shot to death in Las Vegas.

Hammer's album *Please Hammer Don't Hurt 'Em* sold fifteen million copies.

Sublime had their roots in Long Beach in the surf/punk scene of the late '80s. The album *40 oz. to Freedom* was produced for under $1,000 and spent fifty weeks on *Billboard*'s Alternative New Artist

Album chart. In 1996 with the album *What I Got,* a fusion of hip-hop and reggae, Sublime went mainstream. Tragically on the eve of the albums release, the lead singer and guitarist Bradley Nowell died of a heroin overdose. He was twenty-eight years old.

A huge swing revival took place in the '90s. The southern California band **Big Bad Voodoo Daddy** formed in 1992 and received national recognition when their signature song "You and Me and Bottle Makes 3 Tonight" appeared on the *Swingers* soundtrack in 1996.

With a strong rock and roll element, the seventeen-piece **Brian Setzer Orchestra** recreates traditional big band music with energy and originality. This LA band started in 1992 and is going strong.

The very influential band **Green Day** has opened doors to many pop-punk, ska-rock skater metal bands with their release of *Dookie.*

Counting Crows began performing in coffeehouses in San Francisco. Their album *August and Everything After* sold six million copies.

And the list goes on! Other hugely successful California bands of the nineties are **Red Hot Chili Peppers, Beck, Rage Against the Machine, Hole, Blind Melon, No Doubt,** and **Sugar Ray** singing one of my favorite singles, "Someday."

The Final Word

CALIFORNIA LIVING. What does it mean? California is a place where anything goes and nothing stays the same for long. It can be both sophisticated and provincial, cultured and tacky, progressive and unenlightened, violent and unhealthy, or safe and clean. We can become lost and not see another living soul in a dense forest or become so overwhelmed by congestion that we feel we can no longer breathe. It is exactly this kind of diversity, these kinds of contradictions, that keep California from being two things it will never be—ordinary and mundane. Living in a state where everyone thinks the same and everything looks alike has never been the California way.

The facts, opinions, quirks, tales, and stories accumulated here suggest a particular way of living—but there's more. The feeling that we live with, the magic that circulates in the air, is the sense that anything can happen in California. This state is a testing ground, a place where people are free to experiment, to shake things up. Californians are willing to lead the way to places that were previously unfashionable to go.

California has so many resources in such abundance that it doesn't occur that we would not be able to accomplish great things. We have great ambititious dreams and because of the circumstances that are afforded here, those dreams can become reality. Significant historical contributions have come from the people in this state and yet those people are free spirits. We may live a relaxed lifestyle in a naturally casual state but some of the most formidable challenges that the world faces have been conquered by Californians—the same folks that are up at dawn jogging or surfing at sundown.

Because of our nonconformity, our reputation accrues both positive and negative connotations. It is common for others to roll their eyes in a dismissive way at the mention of "a Californian." Because of all the alternative lifestyles that are practiced and an overall different way of doing things, there are those who do not take us seriously. But look at all we have accomplished. And for all that some dismiss, why then do so many continue to flock to California?

Consider all that California offers to the imaginations of people around the world. California represents the good life; we epitomize the American dream. We who live here are aware of this advance billing and there is an arrogance, a California attitude, that goes along with it. We live with it every day. But it cannot be denied that because of a place called California and people known as Californians the world is a different place. We are spirited individuals who dare to be different, to make things happen in an unparalleled fashion, and we pride ourselves on those very things. What prophet among us could have imagined the changes the last hundred years has seen?

California beckons to so many that our population continues to double every eighteen years. Many of us born here refuse to ever leave. With thirty-two and half million people living here, it is not always easy. Making it here is even more difficult because we set our standards impossibly high. It is probably safe to say that more people who come in search of their dream do not find it than those who do. But the saddest words are "it might have been," and what matters is that we tried at all.

What is it then about calling California home that strings a common thread between us? I think it is this:

There a few things in this world that, without exception, every human being does the same. We all must eat and we all must breathe, and from the beginning of time to this very day, every single one of us dreams.

If your desire is to be a world-class athlete, it can be done it California; to traverse a high mountain peak, it can be done in California. If your ambition is to become a star, we have proximity to one of the most important art forms of the twentieth century—the entertainment industry. California dangles glitz and glamour. It can happen here. If your desires are in engineering or technology—the possibilities that were once attributed only to fiction have become a reality in the Silicon Valley. California beckons with the lure of fortune. It can happen here.

There is such vast abundance of opportunity available in California that this dream of a better life is the universal factor that has transcended the passage of time. We feel like we have the world in the palm of our hand because the world keeps coming to us.

California represents the rainbow's end where a fresh new start can be made. With our location comes an expectation of something curious and remarkable located out at the furthest edge of the New World, where the sun always shines and anything is possible. Dreams do come true, although many fade, and the same stars that rise can fall, but one thing is certain—without our dreams we have nothing at all.

The Californian Bill of Rights

We the people of California, in order to fully exploit our residency in the best state of the union, and to provide for and nurture the unique and indomitable spirit of its residents, reserve the following inalienable rights:

1. To use the words "like" and "dude" in every sentence.

2. To take two months off work to find an apartment.

3. To consider earthquakes as weather.

4. To know the difference between "non fat" and "fat free."

5. To own a wetsuit, kayak, snowboard, surfboard, a mountain of camping gear, and at least one article of Gore-Tex clothing.

6. To "telecommute" to work, especially if it's sunny.

7. To know the difference between a French baguette, rustic Italian loaf, foccacia and ciabatta breads.

8. To know the definition of "burl-wood."

9. To never actually park in your garage.

10. To wear shorts to the office.

11. To spend more money on therapy than groceries.

12. To cancel important social plans if you have a good parking space.

13. To know the benefit of all essential oils used in aromatherapy.

14. To order garlic french fries instead of hotdogs at a baseball game.

15. To pay two hundred dollars to be covered with mud by a total stranger.

16. To use fifteen or more words to order a cup of coffee.

17. To never have an empty guestroom.

18. To vacation at home.

19. To call yourself a Californian, even if you came from somewhere else.

20. To feel sorry for people who live anywhere else.

Sources

WHERE WE CAME FROM

THE SHASTA INDIANS OF CALIFORNIA AND THEIR NEIGHBORS, Elizabeth Renfro, Naturegraph Publishers, 1992; AMERICANS AND THE CALIFORNIA DREAM 1850–1915, Kevin Starr, Oxford University Press, 1973, p.10; CHUMASH, A PICTURE OF THEIR WORLD, Bruce W. Miller, Sand River Press, 1988; NATIVE WAYS: CALIFORNIA INDIAN STORIES AND MEMORIES, Malcom Margolin and Yolanda Montijo, Editors, Heydey Books, 1995; CALIFORNIA: A PLACE, A PEOPLE, A DREAM, Claudia K. Jurmain, James J. Rawls, Editors, Chronicle Books, 1986, p. 55; LEGACY: THE ORANGE COUNTY STORY, Ruth Ellen Taylor, Editor, The Register, Santa Ana, 1980, p. 15; CALIFORNIA PLACES AND HISTORY, Chiara Libero and Susanna Perazzoli, Stewart, Tabori & Chang, 1996; HISTORIC SPOTS IN CALIFORNIA, Mildred Brooke Hoover, et al., fourth edition, Stanford Universtiy Press, 1995; ART OF THE STATE CALIFORNIA, Nancy Friedman, Harry N. Abrams, Inc., 1998; U.S. Congress, House, EXECUTIVE DOCUMENTS, 30th Cong., 2nd sess, 1848, 1:14; CALIFORNIA: LAND OF NEW BEGINNINGS, David Lavender, University of Nebraska Press, 1972, p. 150; CALIFORNIA: A BICENTENNIAL HISTORY, David Lavender, pp. 49; THREE YEARS IN CALIFORNIA, Walter Colton, A.S. Barnes and Co., 1850, p. 246–247; DIARY OF A FORTY-NINER, Chauncey L. Canfield, Editor, Turtle Point Press, 1992, pp. 2, 77–79; THE GOLD RUSH SONG BOOK, compiled by Eleanora Black and Sidney Robertson; Colt Press, 1940; 1000 CALIFORNIA PLACE NAMES, Erwin G. Gudde, Universtiy of California Press, Third edition, 1959; THE STORIES BEHIND SONOMA VALLEY PLACE NAMES, Arthur Dawson, Kulupi Publishing, 1998; LIFE IN A CALIFORNIA MISSION: THE JOURNALS OF JEAN FRANCOIS DE LA PÉROUSE, Heydey Books, 1989, pp. 86–89; THE BLACK WEST, William Loren Katz, Open Hand Publishing Inc., Third Edition, 1987; WOMEN OF THE WEST, Cathy Luchetti and Carol Olwell, Orion Books, 1982

WHERE WE LIVE

CALIFORNIA (HELLO USA), Kathy Pelta, Lerner Publications Company, 1995; CALIFORNIA NEVADA TOUR BOOK, AAA Publishing, 1997; STILL WILD, ALWAYS WILD, Susan Zwinger, Sierra Club Books, 1997, pp. 74, 101–102; THE OTHER CALIFORNIA, Gerald Haslam, University of Nevada Press, 1990, pp. 69–70; CALIFORNIA ALMANAC, James S. Fay, Editor, Pacific Data Resources, 1995, 7th Ed.; CALIFORNIA: A HISTORY, Andrew Rolle, Harlan Davidson, Inc., 1998, Fifth Ed.; ROUTE 66: THE MOTHER ROAD, Michael Wallis, St. Martins Press, 1990, pp. 217, 219, 219, 223; JOHN MUIR: TO YOSEMITE AND BEYOND, Robert Engberg and Donald Wesling, Editors, The University of Utah Press, 1999, pp. 43, 44; CALIFORNIA THE CURIOUS, Ray Reynolds, Bear Flag Books, 1989; THE ORANGE COUNTY REGISTER, "Holdout farm sells to Disney," by Marla Jo Fisher and Jerry Hirsch, August 1, 1998, page 1; EXPLORING THE NORTH COAST, Jonathan Franks, Chronicle Books, 1996; GUINESS BOOK OF WORLD RECORDS, 1998 Edition, Bantam Books; UNIQUE CALIFORNIA: A GUIDE TO THE STATE'S QUIRKS, CHARISMA AND CHARACTER, Richard Harris, John Muir Publications, 1994; MICHELIN CALIFORNIA, Michelin Travel Publications, 1997; ORANGE COUNTY SCENE, Michael C. Kilroy, Team MacPherson Publishing Co., 1997

OUR WORK ETHIC

WHO'S WHO IN CALIFORNIA, The Who's Who Historical Society, 1991; LEGACY: DARING TO CARE, Richard A. Schaefer, Legacy Publishing, 1995, pp. 127, 178; FORBES RICHEST PEOPLE, Jonathan T. Davis, Edited by Jonathan T. Davis, John Wiley & Sons, Inc., 1997; THE ENCYCLOPEDIA OF CALIFORNIA, Editor Somerset Publishers, Inc., 1994

CALIFORNIA CUISINE

CALIFORNIA HOME COOKING: AMERICAN COOKING IN THE CALIFORNIA STYLE, Michele Anna Jordan, The Harvard Common Press, 1997; LANG'S COMPENDIUM OF CULINARY NONSENSE AND TRIVIA, George Lang, Wings Books, 1980; CHEZ PANISSE VEGETABLES, Alice Waters, Harper Collins Publishers, 1996; CHASENS, WHERE HOLLYWOOD DINED, Betty Goodwin, Angel City Press, 1996; LOS ANGELES TIMES MAGAZINE, "Home of L.A.'s Big Dippers," by S. Irene Virbila, October 11, 1998, p. 34; APPETITE FOR LIFE: THE BIOGRAPHY OF JULIA CHILD, Noel Riley Fitch, Anchor Books Doubleday, 1997; WESTWAYS MAGAZINE, AAA Publication, March/April 1999

HOW WE HAVE FUN

CALIFORNIA HAPPENINGS: A GUIDE TO FESTIVALS AND SPECIAL EVENTS IN THE GOLDEN STATE, 1998; THE TOP 10 OF EVERYTHING 1998, Russell Ash, DK Publishing, Inc., 1997; CALIFORNIA BEACHES: THE BEACH BUMS BIBLE, Parke Puterbaugh, Alan Bisbort, Foghorn Press, 1996; LOS ANGELES TIMES MAGAZINE, "Grand Slammer," by Bill Dwyre, January 17, 1999, p. 10; HAUNTED HOUSES OF CALIFORNIA A GHOSTLY GUIDE TO HAUNTED HOUSES AND WANDERING SPIRTIS, Antoinette May, World Wide Publishing/Tetra, 1997; GHOST TOWNS OF THE MOJAVE DESERT, Alan Hensher, California Classic Books, 1991; CALIFORNIA GHOST TOWN TRAILS, Broman and Leadabrand, Gem Guides Book Company, 1985; THE ORANGE COUNTY REGISTER, "Surf's Way Up", by Ron Harris, Thursday, Feb. 18, 1999; THE SURFIN'ARY: A DICTIONARY OF SURFING TERMS AND SURFSPEAK, Trevor Gralle, Ten Speed Press, 1991; AVENUES MAGAZINE, AAA Publication, November/December 1998; CALIFORNIA TRIVIA, compiled by Lucy Poshek and Roger Naylor, Rutledge Hill Press, 1998

ARTS AND EDUCATION

THE DEVELOPMENT AND ORGANIZATION OF EDUCATION IN CALIFORNIA, Charles J. Falk, Harcourt, Brace & World, Inc., 1968; NINETY YEARS OF EDUCATION IN CALIFORNIA, William Warren Ferrier, Sather Gate Book Shop, Berkeley CA., Printed by West Coast Printing Co., Copyright 1937 by William Warren Ferrier; CALIFORNIA COLLEGES AND UNIVERSITIES: A Guide to California's Degree-Granting Postsecondary Institutions and to their Degree, Certificate, and Credential Programs, California Postsecondary Education Commission, 1995; THE INSIDERS GUIDE TO COLLEGES, Edited by the Staff of the Yale Daily News, St. Martin's Griffin, twenty-fifth edition, 1999; POPULAR SCIENCE MAGAZINE, December 1998, p. 82; PROTEST! STUDENT ACTIVISM IN AMERICA, Edited by Julian Foster and Durward Long, William Morrow & Company, 1970; THE SIXTIES: FROM MEMORY TO HISTORY, edited by David Farber, The University of North Carolina Press, 1994; THE SIXTIES: YEARS OF HOPE DAYS OF RAGE, Todd Gitlin, Bantam Books, 1993; GATES OF EDEN: AMERICAN CULTURE IN THE SIXTIES, Morris Dickstein, Harvard University Press, 1997; RICHARD NIXON (ENCYCLOPEDIA OF PRESIDENTS), Dee Lillegard, Childrens Press, 1988; EDUCATIONAL AND CAREER OPPORTUNITIES IN ALTERNATIVE MEDICINE, Rosemary Jones, Prima Publishing, 1998; THE LOS ANGELES TIMES, "A Mountain Man of High Art, Holy Ideas," by Tracy Johnson, Page E2, Thursday, March 4, 1999; LOS ANGELES TIMES, Advertising Supplement, Thursday, March 4, 1999, "The Caltech Story—Research, Exploration, Discovery," By Margo McCall, pp. 1–4; SPANISH SONGS OF OLD CALIFORNIA, Collected and translated by Chas. F. Lummis, Published by Chas. F. Lummis, 1923; THE NEW GROVE DICTIONARY OF AMERICAN MUSIC, Edited by H. Wiley Hitchcock and Stanley Sadie, 1986, Volume III, pp. 107–114 by Robert Stevenson, Volume IV, pp 132–134 by Robert Stevenson, Volume IV, pp. 135–141 by Robert Commanday; CALIFORNIA SOUL: MUSIC OF AFRICAN AMERICANS IN THE WEST, Edited by Jacqueline Cogdell DjeDje and Eddie S. Meadows, University of California Press, 1998; HISTORY OF MUSIC IN SAN FRANCISCO SERIES: FIFTY LOCAL PRODIGEES, 1906–1940, Volume V, Cornel Lengyel, Editor, AMS Press, Inc. 1940; PAINTINGS OF CALIFORNIA, Edited by Arnold Skolnick, Intro. by Ilene Susan Fort, University of California Press, 1993; THE ROLLING STONE ILLUSTRATED HISTORY OF ROCK & ROLL, Anthony DeCurtis and James Henke, Random House, Third Edition, 1992; ARTISTS COMMUNITIES, Tricia Snell, Editor, Alworth Press, 1996; SAN FRANCISCO OPERA: THE FIRST 75 YEARS, Joan Chatfield-Taylor, Chronicle Books, 1997; RONALD REAGAN: Fortieth President of the United States (ENCYCLOPEDIA OF PRESIDENTS), Zachary Kent, Childrens Press, 1989; DAILY BRUIN, Published by ASUCLA Communications Board, Los Angeles, "UCLA computer experts sparked birth of Internet," by Jaime Wilson-Chiru, January 15, 1999, p. 1.

About the Author

Heather Waite is a second-generation California native. Born and raised in Orange County, she has also lived in West Hollywood, Silverlake, Beverly Hills, Malibu, and Pacific Palisades.

Heather is a certified substance abuse counselor from UCLA and is currently working toward a Ph.D. in psychology at Ryokan College in Los Angeles. Her volunteer work has included finding sober living environments for the homeless and chemically dependent, and working with people with schizophrenia.

A former Miss Orange County, Heather has traveled around the world as an international model, appeared on television shows and in commercials, and previously worked in the entertainment industry. She has faithfully maintained a daily journal for twenty-three years, completed a memoir, and studied creative writing. Heather has written and published magazine and newspaper articles and plans to combine her love of writing with her psychotherapy practice to be a writer/psychologist. This is her first published book.

About the Press

Wildcat Canyon Press publishes books that embrace such subjects as friendship, spirituality, women's issues, and home and family, all with a focus on self-help and personal growth. Great care is taken to create books that inspire reflection and improve the quality of our lives. Our books invite sharing and are frequently given as gifts.

For a catalog of our publications, please write:

WILDCAT CANYON PRESS
2716 Ninth Street
Berkeley, California 94710
Phone: (510) 848-3600
Fax: (510) 848-1326
info@wildcatcanyon.com

More Wildcat Canyon titles . . .

Calling the Midwest Home: A Lively Look at the Origins, Attitudes, Quirks and Curiosities of America's Heartland
A somewhat irreverent (but always loving) look at the people who call the Midwest home—whether they live there or not. First in the Calling It Home™ series.
Carolyn Lieberg
$14.95 ISBN 1-885171-12-9

Those Who Can . . . Teach!: Celebrating Teachers Who Make a Difference
A tribute to our nation's teachers!
Lorraine Glennon and Mary Mohler
$12.95 ISBN 1-885171-35-8

A Couple of Friends: The Remarkable Friendship between Straight Women and Gay Men
What makes the friendships between straight women and gay men so wonderful? Find out in this honest and fascinating book.
Robert H. Hopcke and Laura Rafaty
$14.95 ISBN 1-885171-33-1

Still Friends: Living Happily Ever After . . . Even If Your Marriage Falls Apart
True stories of couples who have managed to keep their friendships intact after splitting up.
Barbara Quick
$12.95 ISBN 1-885171-36-6

girlfriends: Invisible Bonds, Enduring Ties
Filled with true stories of ordinary women and extraordinary friendships, girlfriends *has become a gift of love among women everywhere.*
Carmen Renee Berry and Tamara Traeder
$12.95 ISBN 1-885171-08-0
ALSO AVAILABLE: Hardcover gift edition, $20.00 ISBN 1-885171-20-X

girlfriends Talk About Men: Sharing Secrets for a Great Relationship
This book shares insights from real women in real relationships— not just from the "experts."
Carmen Renee Berry and Tamara Traeder
$14.95 ISBN 1-885171-21-8

girlfriends for life: Friendships Worth Keeping Forever
This follow-up to the best-selling girlfriends *is an all-new collection of stories and anecdotes about the amazing bonds of women's friendships.*
Carmen Renee Berry and Tamara Traeder
$13.95 ISBN 1-885171-32-3

Aunties: Our Older, Cooler, Wiser Friends
An affectionate tribute to the unique and wonderful women we call "Auntie."
Tamara Traeder and Julienne Bennett
$12.95 ISBN 1-885171-22-6

The Courage to be a Stepmom: Finding Your Place Without Losing Yourself
Hands-on advice and emotional support for stepmothers.
Sue Patton Thoele
$14.95 ISBN 1-885171-28-5

Celebrating Family: Our Lifelong Bonds with Parents and Siblings
True stories about how baby boomers have recognized the flaws of their families and come to love them as they are.
Lisa Braver Moss
$13.95 ISBN 1-885171-30-7

Independent Women: Creating Our Lives, Living Our Visions
How women value independence and relationship and are redefining their lives to accommodate both.
Debra Sands Miller
$16.95 ISBN 1-885171-25-0

The Worrywart's Companion: Twenty-one Ways to Soothe Yourself and Worry Smart
The perfect gift for anyone who lies awake at night worrying.
Dr. Beverly Potter
$11.95 ISBN 1-885171-15-3

Books are available at fine bookstores nationwide.
Prices subject to change without notice.